Online Resources

Access practical templates of the concepts that you will learn in this book as part of the online resources. These downloadable templates will help you implement your learnings in the real world and give you an in-depth understanding of the concepts. The templates include:

1. Business Planner

2. Porter's Five Forces Analysis Worksheet

3. Business introduction letter template

To access the templates, follow the steps below:

1. Go to **www.vibrantpublishers.com**

2. Click on the **'Online Resources'** option on the Home Page

3. Login by entering your account details (or create an account if you don't have one)

4. Go to the Self-Learning Management series section and click on the **'Entrepreneurship Essentials You Always Wanted To Know'** link and access the templates.

Happy self-learning!

This page is intentionally left blank

SELF-LEARNING MANAGEMENT SERIES

VIBRANT
PUBLISHERS

ENTREPRENEURSHIP ESSENTIALS

YOU ALWAYS WANTED TO KNOW

Learn the fundamentals of becoming a skillful and successful entrepreneur

DR. ANNAMARIA BLIVEN

Entrepreneurship Essentials You Always Wanted To Know
First Edition

Paperback ISBN 10: 1-63651-160-0
Paperback ISBN 13: 978-1-63651-160-3

Ebook ISBN 10: 1-63651-161-9
Ebook ISBN 13: 978-1-63651-161-0

Hardback ISBN 10: 1-63651-162-7
Hardback ISBN 13: 978-1-63651-162-7

Library of Congress Control Number: 2023930730

This publication is designed to provide accurate and authoritative information in regard to the subject matter covered. The Author has made every effort in the preparation of this book to ensure the accuracy of the information. However, information in this book is sold without warranty either expressed or implied. The Author or the Publisher will not be liable for any damages caused or alleged to be caused either directly or indirectly by this book.

Vibrant Publishers books are available at special quantity discount for sales promotions, or for use in corporate training programs. For more information please write to bulkorders@vibrantpublishers.com

Please email feedback / corrections (technical, grammatical or spelling) to spellerrors@vibrantpublishers.com

To access the complete catalogue of Vibrant Publishers, visit www.vibrantpublishers.com

SELF-LEARNING MANAGEMENT SERIES

TITLE	PAPERBACK* ISBN

ACCOUNTING, FINANCE & ECONOMICS

COST ACCOUNTING AND MANAGEMENT ESSENTIALS	9781636511030
FINANCIAL ACCOUNTING ESSENTIALS	9781636510972
FINANCIAL MANAGEMENT ESSENTIALS	9781636511009
MACROECONOMICS ESSENTIALS	9781636511818
MICROECONOMICS ESSENTIALS	9781636511153
PERSONAL FINANCE ESSENTIALS	9781636511849

ENTREPRENEURSHIP & STRATEGY

BUSINESS PLAN ESSENTIALS	9781636511214
BUSINESS STRATEGY ESSENTIALS	9781949395778
ENTREPRENEURSHIP ESSENTIALS	9781636511603

GENERAL MANAGEMENT

BUSINESS LAW ESSENTIALS	9781636511702
DECISION MAKING ESSENTIALS	9781636510026
LEADERSHIP ESSENTIALS	9781636510316
PRINCIPLES OF MANAGEMENT ESSENTIALS	9781636511542
TIME MANAGEMENT ESSENTIALS	9781636511665

*Also available in Hardback & Ebook formats

SELF-LEARNING MANAGEMENT SERIES

TITLE	PAPERBACK* ISBN
HUMAN RESOURCE MANAGEMENT	
DIVERSITY IN THE WORKPLACE ESSENTIALS	9781636511122
HR ANALYTICS ESSENTIALS	9781636510347
HUMAN RESOURCE MANAGEMENT ESSENTIALS	9781949395839
ORGANIZATIONAL BEHAVIOR ESSENTIALS	9781636510378
ORGANIZATIONAL DEVELOPMENT ESSENTIALS	9781636511481
MARKETING & SALES MANAGEMENT	
DIGITAL MARKETING ESSENTIALS	9781949395747
MARKETING MANAGEMENT ESSENTIALS	9781636511788
SALES MANAGEMENT ESSENTIALS	9781636510743
SERVICES MARKETING ESSENTIALS	9781636511733
OPERATIONS & PROJECT MANAGEMENT	
AGILE ESSENTIALS	9781636510057
OPERATIONS & SUPPLY CHAIN MANAGEMENT ESSENTIALS	9781949395242
PROJECT MANAGEMENT ESSENTIALS	9781636510712
STAKEHOLDER ENGAGEMENT ESSENTIALS	9781636511511

*Also available in Hardback & Ebook formats

About the Author

Dr. AnnaMaria Bliven has worked as a business professional for over 30 years gaining experience in business development and management, business improvement, project management, career development and advancement, business strategy, vet-entrepreneurship, team development, teaching and training, and implementation of community projects, and many more lessons learned in starting and sustaining for-profit and not-for-profit businesses.

As a seasoned business owner, her goals are to share lessons and best practices for starting, sustaining, and succeeding in business ventures. To that end, she meets with clients on a regular basis assisting them with achieving their career and business goals. Dr. Bliven started her career as a Certified Travel Consultant while in the Army National Guard and served a total of 26 years with combined service in the Army National Guard, Army, and Army Reserve in the career fields of music, human resources, and education services, and career development. She achieved her Certification as a Global Career Development Facilitator in addition to becoming a Data Analyst and a college instructor. She has an undergraduate degree in Communication from Arizona State University, a Master of Arts degree in Communication from West Virginia University, a Master's in Business Administration from Colorado Technical University-online, and a Doctorate in Business Administration from the University of Wisconsin-Whitewater.

Other Contributors

Julie A. DeSot, DM, has a Doctorate in Management from the University of Maryland Global Campus. She has over ten years of instructional experience and 26 years of professional experience in leadership, management, and project/program management. Dr. DeSot helps individuals and organizations improve their performance through process improvement, professional development, and consulting. She also has professional memberships in Project Management Institute (PMI) and MyAxelos.

What experts say about this book!

The book "Entrepreneurship Essentials You Always Wanted To Know" by Vibrant Publishers covers various aspects of entrepreneurship, from the history of the field to the legal structures relevant to different types of businesses and entrepreneurs. One of the strengths of the book is its emphasis on differentiating between starting a product-based and a service-based business. This is an important distinction as the two types of businesses require different strategies and approaches to be successful.

Another strength of the book is its focus on creating a value proposition, which is a critical step in developing a business idea that meets the needs of the market. Additionally, the book provides a good overview of the legal structures relevant to different types of businesses and entrepreneurs, which can be a confusing and overwhelming topic for many entrepreneurs.

The book's coverage of the stage beyond startup is also noteworthy, as it focuses on running and managing a company, as well as growing the business through innovation. This is a crucial area for entrepreneurs to understand, as many startups fail in the post-startup phase.

Overall, "Entrepreneurship Essentials You Always Wanted To Know" by Vibrant Publishers is a valuable resource for aspiring and established entrepreneurs looking to enhance their knowledge and skills.

– Arkadiusz Mironko, Associate Professor of Management and Entrepreneurship, Indiana University East

The author has covered all the essential topics about entrepreneurship in this book in a simple and easy to understand language. This will be a resourceful book for undergraduate and graduate courses and also for new entrepreneurs.

– Bharath Samishetti, Assistant Professor, Balaji Institute of Management Sciences

What experts say about this book!

Entrepreneurship Essentials is a must-read book for anyone ever interested in entrepreneurship. It dispels the stereotype that all entrepreneurs are billionaire college drop-outs hailing from Silicon Valley and is instead applicable for anyone seeking to start and grow any kind of enterprise both profit and non-profit. In addition, it would be an interesting read for managers and leaders of large firms interested in creating a more entrepreneurial culture in a world of increased global competition and technology transformation. I highly recommend it.

– David Fogarty, Chief Marketing Analytics and Data and Technology Officer, Evernorth Corporation

This book covers all aspects of entrepreneurship and is compact, hence readable and approachable.

– Naeem Zafar, Professor-of-the-Practice & Faculty Director, San Francisco Campus

This is a very easy read to acquaint first-year business students with the concept of entrepreneurship. The chapters covered the basics of business ownership, from company formation to marketing. The self-check quizzes at the end of each chapter were helpful.

– Dr. D. Zaharopoulos, Business Faculty, Phoenix College

Table of Contents

Preface

Entrepreneurship is one of the buzzwords that often turn people's heads when they hear it. This is because names like Elon Musk, Mukesh Ambani, Oprah Winfrey, Bill Gates, and others fill everyone with the excitement that the word "entrepreneurship" is synonymous with "wealth". So, is entrepreneurship truly a force for good and a possible pathway to making money?

If you are wondering how to find suitable answers to that very important question or discover how you could become an entrepreneur yourself, *Entrepreneurship Essentials You Always Wanted To Know* is the only guide on entrepreneurship that you would ever need. This book delves into the basics or fundamentals of entrepreneurship—who are "entrepreneurs", what they do, how they do it, possible outcomes they get, and how they improve their activities.

Entrepreneurship, for the most part, is about building a business or a company, establishing operational systems, and steering it to success. that will eventually bring that fantastic "wealth" that most people associate with entrepreneurship. *Entrepreneurship Essentials* will take you through this fascinating "entrepreneurship journey" so that when you eventually finish it, you will be almost ready to take the jump into building your first business!

This page is intentionally left blank

Introduction to the book

As popular as the word "entrepreneurship" is, it is uninspiring that very few people understand the nitty-gritties of how to set up and successfully run a business or company. Apart from business schools or business/commerce departments in universities where students learn some aspects of entrepreneurship, there are very few opportunities for would-be entrepreneurs to learn about the trade. Entrepreneurship is a demanding profession that requires a set of both hard and soft skills and some practical knowledge.

Worse still, not many books out there address all the necessary areas or aspects of entrepreneurship that an aspiring business owner should have deep knowledge of. This is why *Entrepreneurship Essentials You Always Wanted To Know* is written to bridge the knowledge gap and provide detailed information about what it takes to successfully start and manage a company.

After you have completed reading this book, you will have a profound understanding of the following aspects of entrepreneurship:

- Who are entrepreneurs, and how you can become a goal-getting business owner.

- Understanding your "Big Idea" and establishing a business/company to bring your big idea to life (to the world).

- What are your products/services and how you can position them in a way that consumers will want them at all costs. (If you don't sell your products/services, you won't make money!)

- Techniques for knowing your markets and customers inside out and keeping competitors at bay.

- Creating a business model that will stand the test of time and make your business sustainable for a very long time.

- Living your dreams as an entrepreneur and enjoying all the trappings that come with being a successful business owner.

Who can benefit from this book?

One great benefit of this book is that it will provide readers with all the necessary and significant information about entrepreneurship and teach them how to turn their big ideas into profitable businesses/companies.

Who can benefit from this book?

- **Students:** Students who want to know more about entrepreneurship can find this book invaluable, whether they are in high school, university, or business school.

- **Entrepreneurs/Business owners:** Those who are currently running their own businesses can use this book as a practical guide which they can consult daily to obtain improved methodologies that they can use in order to give their businesses new directions.

- **Academics:** University professors can use this book to supplement their teachings on entrepreneurship. Their students will derive immense knowledge of company formation, structure, and operations from it.

- **Managers/Organizers of trade or business organizations:** The gem of information about business management in this book can be utilized by organizations to instruct their members (who are business owners) in periodic business events, workshops, seminars, symposia, and others

- **Directors/Managers of Incubators, Business Development Centers, and Business Bootcamps:** This book offers new perspectives on entrepreneurship that can be taught to participants of business boot camps, incubation, and business development.

This page is intentionally left blank

How to use the book?

Whether you are an existing business owner looking to get more knowledge about entrepreneurship or currently in business school or college learning about entrepreneurship, this book is designed in a way that you could make use of the actionable steps provided in it. The goal is to help you have a deep understanding of what entrepreneurship entails and how you can become an entrepreneur yourself if you so desire.

- So, approach this book with an open mind: You will find many interesting facts, tips, case studies, and highlights that might challenge what you already knew or had been taught about entrepreneurship. This book simplifies entrepreneurship so that even high school students can understand the topic; however, you will unearth practical advice and revelations in it

- Take notes, ask questions, and investigate all assumptions raised in the book. By doing this, you won't only get familiarized with the essential issues addressed in the book but eventually master them

- This book is useful for those who organize business meetings, symposia, and other events where they brainstorm about how to become better business owners. So, introduce this book to your business partners, friends, and classmates.

This page is intentionally left blank

Chapter **1**

Who Are Entrepreneurs and Why Do You Want to Be One?

One of the most accurate definitions of "an entrepreneur" is found in the Oxford Dictionary, which states that "an entrepreneur is a person who makes money by starting or running a business, especially when this involves taking financial risks." Two important and relatively interdependent factors are mentioned in this concise, but self-explanatory definition: Entrepreneurship is all about making money while taking calculated financial risks. Those two actions go hand-in-hand. In other words, you stand a little chance of creating wealth for yourself and your future generation if you shy away from taking some business risks.

Key learning objectives should include the reader's understanding of the following:

- Entrepreneurs as business owners and/or problem-solvers

- Five (5) qualities/attributes every entrepreneur must have

- Entrepreneurship checklists to determine your readiness to become an entrepreneur

- Why some entrepreneurs succeed and others don't

1.1 Entrepreneurs Are Business Owners and/or Problem-Solvers

Entrepreneurs are business owners or managers of businesses. They either set up their own businesses from scratch, purchase existing businesses, or partner with owners of other businesses through the acquisition of equity. On the other hand, an entrepreneur may not own a business of his/her own but help another person or a group of people manage their businesses. In both cases, an entrepreneur's primary responsibilities are to direct the affairs of the business, oversee its day-to-day operations, and steer it toward consistent profitability.

Fun facts about entrepreneurs

- 88% of millionaires in the United States are self-made entrepreneurs (Wealth-X)

- There are about 582 million entrepreneurs around the globe (The Hill)

- 90% of new American billionaires are self-made business owners (Forbes)

1.1.1 Business as a Force for Good

Businesses are established to solve the numerous problems that people have in our world. If you want to cut your hair but don't have the equipment to do so, a barber on the corner of your street can help you. In the same way, clothing factories are built to make comfortable materials that we can use to cover ourselves, and schools are founded so that we can all be properly educated.

It is clear from the examples provided above that businesses are actually a force for good! According to Paul Marsden, "business is all about solving people's problems—at a profit." Even though most entrepreneurs hope to make money from their businesses, they don't set out to create cash-making machines from the onset. What they want to do is to solve a particular problem by establishing a company that will offer the necessary solutions to the problem(s).

1.1.2 Entrepreneurs as Problem-Solvers

It is somehow a misconception for someone to set out to establish a company for the singular purpose of making money from it. Even though there is nothing wrong with becoming wealthy by owning a business, if that's the sole reason a person goes into business, t he/she may become frustrated in the process of running such a business. As it will be shown in this book, successfully running a business requires a set of skills, dedication, and hard work. Without putting in enough effort, such a wealth-seeking entrepreneur is putting himself/herself up for a colossal failure.

That aside, well-intentioned, hardworking entrepreneurs are actually problem-solvers. When the world needed an efficient cell phone, Apple, Inc., led by the visionary Steve Jobs came up with the iPhone; when people were tired of going to malls to shop every time, Jeff Bezos' Amazon was born.

1.2 Five Qualities/Attributes Every Entrepreneur Must Have

It is not an overstatement that entrepreneurs are a unique breed of human beings. They possess some specific qualities that are uncommon among other groups of people. Five of these admirable qualities include:

1. **Risk-taking attitude:** Setting up and smoothly running a company is all about taking calculated risks. Elon Musk's friend once compared it with *"eating glass and staring into the abyss."* This comparison is not far from the truth. When you are starting a business, you probably don't know how it is going to end, whether it will survive or collapse like thousands of other businesses that close shop every year. Unfortunately, not many people are comfortable taking the amount of risks that entrepreneurs are willing to take. This is the primary reason there are very few entrepreneurs in the world. It is natural for people to play safe when it comes to investing their money, time, and other resources. Entrepreneurs, on the other hand, don't act like that—they will go all in until they succeed or learn some cogent lessons about entrepreneurship.

2. **Passionate about what they do:** A company can't run itself; it needs capable and passionate people to manage its affairs. As an entrepreneur, you cannot be passive about running

your business's day-to-day activities. You must be all in, utilizing all the financial and operational resources at your disposal. Entrepreneurs, through dedication and hard work, will systematically confront any challenges that may be threatening their businesses' chances of survival. Some of the challenges may be daunting and sometimes not under the control of the entrepreneurs. Take for instance, when the interest rate is suddenly raised or lowered when the inflation bites harder than expected, or if wars break out in some parts of the world. All those events or occurrences are beyond what an entrepreneur can control. However, instead of panicking or worrying about the enormity of the unexpected challenges, astute entrepreneurs will sit down and strategize how to mitigate the impacts of such problems and save their businesses from a sudden collapse. Having a vision is important, but it is a strong passion for what one is doing that will drive the vision. If you don't like your business or the industry you are operating in, it is almost impossible for you to be visionary with the kinds of products/services you are offering in the industry. So, being passionate about your calling as an entrepreneur is a desirable attribute.

3. **Hard working:** It is obvious that entrepreneurship is not for the weak-hearted. This is because it requires a lot of work. Business owners divide a great deal of their scarce time and other resources protecting their businesses as well as finding strategic ways to increase profitability through offering high-quality products/services that customers will like and continue to patronize. This quantity of work that entrepreneurs put into their companies takes time; it is not rare for some business owners to put in as many as 70-80 hours a week to achieve great success in their

entrepreneurship pursuits. Sometimes they work overnight or even get up very early in the morning to work. Becoming a successful business owner isn't a sprint—it is indeed a marathon! What matters is what you do from time to time to keep your business active and prospering. This will take your time, energy, and complete dedication. Companies or businesses, on several occasions, have been compared to entrepreneurs' babies. As such, good parents must sacrifice a lot for their offspring's needs, even if it means denying themselves some pleasures.

4. **Resilient and flexible:** Most of the progressive entrepreneurs in the world today are known to be resilient and flexible. This entails that whatever circumstances occur to their businesses, they do not let them confuse or perplex them. Instead, they choose to remain calm and collected while planning appropriate solutions to the problems that their companies may be facing. In entrepreneurship, there are no hard rules; every rule is there to be broken. So, business owners must exhibit a high level of flexibility in situations surrounding their companies that are not within their power to control. This is to say that someone who often worries or fidgets about things may not be suitable for entrepreneurship because many unexpected problems will push such a person into having health issues, like hypertension or heart attack. A resilient business owner understands the fact that no condition is permanent and every storm will soon pass. During their dark times, experienced business owners will network with their business associates or partners, make new connections, and deploy both financial and human resources to sail their companies from troubled waters.

5. **Confident:** As an entrepreneur, you must exude strong self-confidence and self-esteem. Your employees, business partners, and even customers are watching you. They will reflect whatever you show them. A business owner that often looks troubled and worried will dampen the confidence of everyone around him/her. His/her employees will be scared to do exploits or make any risky moves on behalf of the company. They will be afraid to make any decisions they think may contradict their boss's opinions. This situation will cause confusion and slow the progress in such a company since the prevailing environment in the company does not encourage taking risks and being innovative.

Figure 1.1   **5 Qualities/Attributes of an entrepreneur**

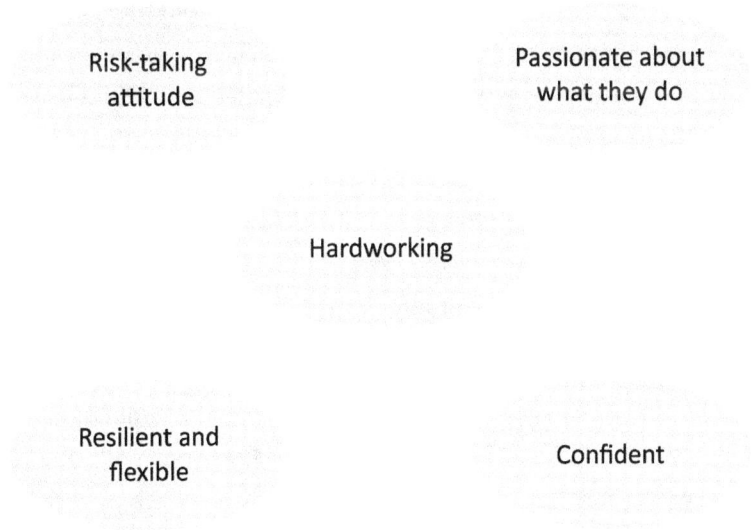

Risk-taking
attitude

Passionate about
what they do

Hardworking

Resilient and
flexible

Confident

1.3 Are You Ready to Jump on the Entrepreneurship Bandwagon?

There may not be a direct answer to this all-important question. People become entrepreneurs for different reasons. If your responses to three of the four questions below are in the affirmative "YES", you may consider entrepreneurship as your future endeavor:

- **Do you want to bring a positive change to the world?** Creating a business is not all about money. According to Peter Drucker, *"the entrepreneur always searches for change, responds to it, and exploits it as an opportunity."* What do you think needs to change? Have you spotted some aspects of our health, education, or justice system that are ripe for disruption? When people realized that fossil fuel is making our planet dirty, they came up with electric vehicles; during the pandemic, when people were locked behind their doors, online schooling and meetings became the norm; and the rate at which people embraced online shopping skyrocketed! All these are needful changes that our world requires at this moment. What kind of change are you hoping to introduce to the world?

- **Are you good at working with or managing people?** No one is an island—this entails that you cannot manage your company alone. You will be required to work with others who share in your lofty dreams. Mary Kay Ash once said, "a company is only as good as the people it keeps." An entrepreneur who doesn't have the people skill or team spirit may find himself/herself destroying the company he/she has built.

- **Can you handle adversities?** No smooth sailing is promised in business. All sorts of unexpected or unimaginable problems may crop up while managing your business. Are you able to weather all these hurdles? If you are the type that gets frustrated when things are not going your way, you may be unfit to become an entrepreneur. Robert Kiyosaki, the author of "Rich Dad, Poor Dad" said, *"when times are bad is when the real entrepreneurs emerge"*. With the help of your employees, you should be able to steer your company away from dangers anytime unforeseen challenges show up.

- **Can you sell?** After making your ground-breaking products or creating your wonderful services, you will still need to sell them. Without getting repeated sales from happy and loyal customers, your business may not have enough revenue to keep its doors open. If you cannot sell things by yourself, are you able to assemble a team of self-motivated salespeople who will put your products in front of those who will be willing to pay for them? W. Edwards Deming reportedly said, *"profit in business comes from repeat customers, customers that boast about your project or service, and that bring friends with them."*

1.4 Entrepreneurship Checklist to Consider

Anyone can become an entrepreneur, whether college-educated or not. However, not everyone has what it takes to set up a business, manage it successfully, and profit from it. Today, it is inspiring to see that most rich people on Bloomberg's Billionaire List are entrepreneurs. However, they have contributed time, effort, financial resources, and everything they have got to make their businesses succeed. You can do that, too, if you are cut out to be an entrepreneur!

This checklist is meant to remind you about the necessary attributes an entrepreneur should possess. More so, it gives you the unique opportunity to carry out some self-assessment to see whether you are capable of becoming an entrepreneur.

NOTE: How to use the checklist below

Action: Award any score from 1-10 to each question. 1 being the least score and 10 the most.

Results: If your total score is 50 or more, you have what it takes to be an entrepreneur.

If your total score is 49 or less, you are not naturally cut out to be an entrepreneur but you can improve your skills.

Table 1.1 Entrepreneurship checklist to determine your readiness to become an entrepreneur

No.	Question	Awarded score
1	To what extent can you act under pressure?	
2	Do you see yourself as a risk-taker?	
3	How much of a team worker are you?	
4	Do you like delegating duties to others?	
5	Are you a hard-working person?	
6	Do you feel optimistic no matter what?	

7	How quickly can you find a solution to any problem?
8	Do you learn from mentors and people who have experienced what you are trying to do?
9	Do you exude a positive and friendly personality?
10	How short-lived is your anger?
	Total Score

1.5 Why Some Entrepreneurs Succeed and Others Don't

Starting a business is the same as starting a journey. A blog from Entrepreneurship in a Box said it best - "Business is just a simple start of a long journey into the world of equations with many unknowns" (Sutevski, 2023). It is the fear of the unknowns that at times paralyze someone starting a business and as such has moments of indecision, doubt in their abilities, and loss of control.

Successful entrepreneurs have four factors in common.

1. They invest time, talent, and treasure into creativity, establishing characteristics, and communication of their business regardless of bad days. Creativity and innovation are the foundation of the business and feed the purpose and existence of the business. Establishing the characteristics of a business is what gives the business life and attractiveness. These are the unique benefits and features that clients

and customers will enjoy as they receive the product or service the business offers. Communication in the form of marketing is a must and successful entrepreneurs consistently and constantly broadcast their existence and the successful outcomes to their clients and customers.

2. Successful entrepreneurs exhibit perseverance which is the key to keep moving forward, even in moments when it seems the business may be failing. They may reach out to partners or investors when the business may not be doing good financially. They take immediate action and are able to persuade others to join them either as a joint venture or to add venture capital.

3. Failure is not an option. The philosophy of knowing where there is a will, there is a way is part of the mantra of the moment when it may seem the business is about to fall apart. In situations like these, instead of panicking, good entrepreneurs focus on what went wrong. Problem-solving is their first instinct and not the temptation to close the business. There are many stories of successful entrepreneurs who faced moments that seemed like the business was failing, and were able to think clearly, get creative, and take action to save the business from collapsing.

4. Successful business owners are always seeking information and knowledge from fellow business owners, retired business owners, etc to assist with moments when the business needs these resources for whatever reason. These successful entrepreneurs have a vast network of colleagues, professionals, friends, and acquaintances. They invite feedback, act on it constantly look for ways to improve.

Quiz

1. According to the Oxford Dictionary, an entrepreneur is someone who_____

   a. starts a business and makes money from it

   b. goes to a business school

   c. buys products made by other businesses and uses them

2. What percentage of millionaires in the United States are self-made entrepreneurs?

   a. 65%

   b. 70%

   c. 88%

3. The following are attributes of an astute business owner except_____

   a. risk-taking

   b. laziness

   c. self-confidence

4. What is the estimated number of entrepreneurs around the world?

   a. 100 million

   b. 582 million

   c. 82 million

5. **Why is an entrepreneur expected to be flexible?**

   a. Sometimes, things may not go as planned.

   b. They should never be flexible.

   c. I don't know.

6. **Mr. James loves taking calculated financial risks and is highly self-motivated; Mr. Alan is a lazy and fearful man who doesn't like trying something new. Which of these two men will become a better entrepreneur?**

   a. Mr. Alan

   b. Mr. James

   c. I don't know

7. **What percentage of new American billionaires are self-made entrepreneurs?**

   a. 50%

   b. 90%

   c. 10%

8. **What does this expression mean: "Businesses are all about great relationships"?**

   a. It means that an entrepreneur needs to foster good relationships with his/her employees, customers, and business associates.

   b. It is not necessary that an entrepreneur should be friendly with anyone.

   c. I don't know.

9. **To be regarded as someone who has a wonderful team spirit,_____.**

    a. you must be able to fight everyone you work with.

    b. you should be able to perform well within a team.

    c. you shouldn't bother yourself about teams.

10. **Most successful business owners have mentors who guide them in entrepreneurship.**

    a. True

    b. False

    c. I don't know

Answers	1 – a	2 – c	3 – b	4 – b	5 – a
	6 – b	7 – b	8 – a	9 – b	10 – a

Chapter Summary

◆ Entrepreneurship is not for everyone. It is only those who are ready to give what it takes that can be successful at it.

◆ Entrepreneurs should be perceived as a force for good because they bring innovative solutions to the world's problems.

◆ Five main attributes displayed by goal-getting business owners are - a risk-taking attitude, passionate, hard working, resilient and flexible, and confident

◆ To perform in an outstanding manner, an entrepreneur must have a sensible purpose for starting his/her business besides making money.

◆ Entrepreneurship is hard; only fearless and self-motivating individuals can make remarkable success in it

References

- Jose de la Torre, J. "Who Is An Entrepreneur?" Enterpreneur. April 30, 2015. Retrieved from www.entrepreneur.com

- Walker, B. "Six Personality Traits of Successful Entrepreneurs." Forbes. May 11, 2020. Retrieved from www.forbes.com

This page is intentionally left blank

Chapter **2**

What is Your Big Business Idea?

Great businesses are built on wonderful and phenomenal ideas or concepts. Any entrepreneur who wants to be a reckoning force or a dominant player in his/her chosen industry must come up with an innovative and transformational idea. This is to say that companies are not established on mere fantasies or unsubstantiated concepts. If your big business idea cannot stand the test of time, the company you are trying to form will crumble like a sandcastle in no time. .

Key learning objectives should include the reader's understanding of the following:

- How necessity brings about innovations

- What are great business opportunities and how to easily identify them

- What are your idea's competitive advantages

2.1 Necessity Brings About Innovations

Human beings have gone through different ages/periods in history as they seek better ways of living and lifestyles. From the Stone Age (that ended between 4,000 BCE and 2,000 BCE) to the Modern Era, human explorers and innovators have worked tirelessly to design tools, devices, equipment, and other materials that have made life easier and more comfortable for everyone.

2.1.1 The Four Industrial Revolutions

In recent times, our world has passed through four distinct industrial revolutions that have dramatically changed the way we live. Each of these industrial revolutions offered exactly what people needed to transform their lives and their environments.

- **First industrial revolution:** This brought about machine production. People stopped using their hands to make things and utilized steam power and water power to drive machines that were employed in manufacturing. This revolution took place between 1760 and 1840.

- **Second industrial revolution:** This is also referred to as the "Technological Revolution" which occurred between 1871 and 1914. During those periods, telegraphic networks were built and extended railroads were installed.

- **Third industrial revolution:** This revolution occurred mainly in the late 20th century after the two world wars that slowed down industrialization and technological advancement. This is also called the "Digital Revolution" because it marked the periods when computers of different complexities were invented and manufactured.

- **Fourth industrial revolution:** We are currently in the Fourth Industrial Revolution, which is also referred to as the "Internet Revolution" or "Information Age". This revolution opens the doors to exploring cloud computing, artificial intelligence, cyber-physical systems (CPS), the Internet of Things (IoTs), and other internet-connected endeavors.

It is clear from all indications that necessities bring about phenomenal innovations in human history. These inventions are based on concrete business ideas that have survived challenging times.

Discussion Question:
During which Industrial Revolution did Thomas Edison invent the light bulb?

2.2 What are Great Business Opportunities and How to Easily Identify Them?

Everyone who wants to become an entrepreneur often wonders where their big business ideas will come from. This is a normal feeling because if you don't come up with a groundbreaking business concept, you may not be able to make a significant impression in the already crowded business world.

So, where do phenomenal business ideas emanate from?

Some astute, world-famous business owners and leaders have answers to this very important question:

- **From your dreams:** Walt Disney, the founder of Disneyland once said, "if you can dream it, you can do it!" What is it that you want to see in the world but no one has invented yet? Get up from your dreaming, scribble the idea down, work on its scopes, and constantly refine the idea until it is ready to be born into the world.

- **As a spark of imagination:** Sometimes, your big business idea may strike you as a spark of imagination. This may come when you are in the bathroom taking a shower or just waking up from bed after a restful night. What do you do if you are in this situation? Here is a piece of advice from Golda Meir, former Israeli Prime Minister, who said, *"make the most of yourself by fanning the tiny, inner sparks of possibility into flames of achievement."* Instead of letting that wonderful inspiration or imagination slip away from your busy mind, do something about it. Run quickly into your room and jot it down in your notebook or journal. When you set aside to work on the idea, it may eventually turn out to be a great business concept.

- **Keep searching:** If you are not fortunate enough to get your great business idea from dreams or as a spark of imagination, you may choose to search for it. A new business concept can be derived from some existing ones. That means you don't have to always worry about getting an entirely new idea that no one has ever dreamt of. You can combine some existing technologies to create an entirely new system that may solve some perennial problems for people.

2.2.1 What are Great Business Opportunities?

A great business opportunity arises from the fact that an entrepreneur has fortunately discovered "a need" that is not yet met and developed products/services that will satisfy that particular need. For example, if you are living in an area where there are few kindergartens for kids from low-income families, you can decide to target that demographic and set up a nursery school that would accommodate children from such families. Similarly, some small towns don't have public libraries where people can go relax and read the latest or new books. If you are concerned about doing good in your community and making money while doing so, you may opt to fill the gap by setting up a private library. Readers can use your private library for a fee.

A shrewd business person understands that when you give customers exactly what they need, they will appreciate your good gestures and return the favor in kind. They will be willing to spend their cash while patronizing the newly established company that is solving some of the problems that they have.

Therefore, good business opportunities are tied to the prospects of solving people's or customers' problems. When the world felt that fossil fuel is polluting our environment and worsening our climate through the headache of global warming, we are presented with electric vehicles.

2.2.2 How to Easily Identify Good Business Opportunities?

There are three significant ways any entrepreneur can identify good business opportunities around them.

1. **Personal complaint:** Do you have something that is bothering you and wondering why it is not yet manufactured by a company? When Bill Bowerman, a former track-and-field coach at the University of Oregon was looking for athletic shoes his students could wear

while running fast, he founded a company with one of his students, Phil Knight in 1964 named Blue Ribbon Sports to produce athletic shoes. The company later rebranded into Nike in 1972.

2. **People's pain points:** If you hang around people for some time you will surely hear them complain about some pain points they are dealing with. They may whine about not having a good plumber, barber, electrician, or even a good babysitter for their little kids. Those are business opportunities.

3. **Product/service extensions:** There are some products that have been designed for certain uses, but consumers want more from the same devices or appliances. It is now for you, an entrepreneur, to create a business on the extra services that people require. For instance, when Apple, Inc made its iPhone, it knew exactly how it wanted people to use the device—for calling, texting, and taking pictures. But iPhone users want to do more with their smartphones, such as playing the piano on it, playing games, or watching live TV programs. To accomplish these extra tasks, other companies designed apps that could be accessed on iPhones for such purposes and now people can do whatever they like on their iPhones, including measuring their heartbeat rates, which was not the original intention of Apple, Inc. for its product!

2.3 What are Your Idea's Competitive Advantages?

It must be stated that not all business ideas are worth developing. If a business concept won't relieve targeted customers of their pain points, it is a waste of time pursuing it.

A business idea is considered very competitive if it has all the following advantages over others:

- **Innovative:** An innovative product or service helps consumers see a better approach for solving a certain problem they have been battling with. When Segway was introduced into the market, people embraced it because it helped them reach their destinations on time by avoiding heavy traffic.

- **Durability:** No one wants to spend their hard-earned money on a product that won't last for some years. If your business idea can't produce a service/product that lasts more than one year (with the exception of common consumables), it is better you refine it and make it durable.

- **Affordability:** If you are not in the luxury industry where products are expected to be a little more expensive than usual, your business idea should be generally affordable. There are some pharmaceutical products that ordinary people cannot buy because they are out of reach for low-income people.

- **Commerciality:** If your products/services won't sell to the point of bringing in profits for your company, it is not competitive enough. People only spend money on products that they need. It doesn't matter how nice your products look, if it lacks commerciality, it will soon result in the collapse of the company you have founded.

Quiz

1. What does the statement "necessity is the mother of all inventions" mean?

   a. People are clueless about how to transform their lives.

   b. When they need something, history reveals that humans have always found a way to make it.

   c. I don't believe inventions are necessary.

2. The First Industrial Revolution led to_____

   a. manual production

   b. machine production

   c. digital production

3. The Second Industrial Revolution is also known as the_____

   a. Digitalization Revolution

   b. Technological Revolution

   c. Internet Revolution

4. The Third Industrial Revolution brought about the_____

   a. cloud computing

   b. digitalizing of things

   c. technological advancement

5. **The Fourth Industrial Revolution is sometimes referred to as the_____**

   a. Information Age

   b. Machine Production Era

   c. Technological Age

6. **The quote, "if you can dream it, you can do it!" is attributed to_____**

   a. Warren Buffett

   b. Mukesh Ambani

   c. Walt Disney

7. **This is NOT one of the recommended ways for an entrepreneur to get a big business idea.**

   a. From dreams

   b. Through sparks of imagination

   c. Stealing someone else's business idea

8. **Albert Einstein once said, "imagination is better than knowledge." How does this statement relate to an entrepreneur?**

   a. It is not compulsory that an entrepreneur should get a college or business school education.

   b. I think Albert Einstein was wrong because knowledge is better than imagination.

   c. I don't know.

9. **The first source of great business ideas for some entrepreneurs are their own_____**

   a. personal complaints

   b. college certificates

   c. family histories

10. **It is believed that by paying attention to people's or others' pain points, an entrepreneur can derive a brilliant business idea from that. What do "pain points" mean in this scenario?**

    a. Problems that people are seeking a solution for

    b. Points you get on your credit card reports

    c. Some points of physical injuries on people's bodies

Answers	1 – b	2 – b	3 – b	4 – b	5 – a
	6 – c	7 – c	8 – a	9 – a	10 – a

Chapter Summary

♦ Necessity, as they say, is the mother of inventions. In human history, people create new tools and materials to make their lives better.

♦ There have been 4 industrial revolutions: First Revolution led to machine production, Second Revolution brought about Technological Revolution, Third Revolution gave birth to the Digitalization Age, and Fourth Revolution gave us the Internet or Information Age

♦ Great business ideas can emanate from dreams, sparks of imagination, and by actively searching for them.

♦ You can identify good business opportunities by paying serious attention to people's pain points, your personal complaints, and requests for new products/services.

♦ A business idea is considered competitive if it is innovative, durable, affordable, and can be commercialized.

References

- Lesonsky, R. "4 Steps To Coming Up With A Great Business Idea." Forbes. March 9, 2019. Retrieved from www.forbes.com

- Tobak, S. "This is Where Big Ideas Come from". Entrepreneur. October 1, 2015. Retrieved from www.entrepreneur.com

This page is intentionally left blank

Chapter **3**

Starting Your Own Company

Setting up a business or a company is the surest way to bring a good business idea into reality. Although not all entrepreneurs opt for this; some prefer to try their ideas, develop them, and sell them outright to an existing company or to another entrepreneur and make small money from that. However, if you want to have firm control over your idea and, of course, its final product for a long time, it is imperative you consider establishing your own company.

Key learning objectives should include the reader's understanding of the following

- Company types and their corresponding legality

- Choosing the best company type

- Company registration and other necessary documentation

3.1 Company Types and Their Corresponding Legality

There are different types of companies or legal business structures that could be set up by entrepreneurs, depending on a number of factors described below:

According to U.S. Small Business Administration (SB (a U.S. Government agency that supports small businesses in America and has local offices all over the country), an entrepreneur can establish any of the legal business structures highlighted as follows:

- **Sole Proprietorship:** You are considered a Sole Proprietorship if you are running a business that is not officially registered. In this scenario, your business assets and liabilities are not separated from your personal assets and liabilities. If the business incurs any debts or liabilities, your personal assets can be used to offset the liabilities. It is possible for you, under the Law, to give your business a trading name as a Sole Proprietor.

- **Partnerships:** This happens to be the simplest legal business structure for two or more people that want to own a business together. The two types of partnerships are (i) Limited Partnerships (LPs), and (ii) Limited Liability Partnerships (LLPs).

  i. **Limited Partnerships (LPs):** LPs are arranged in a way that they have only one general partner with unlimited liability. The other members who have limited liability also have limited control over the company. This arrangement should have been clearly documented in a partnership agreement. For LPs, profits are passed on to members and can be taxed as personal income taxes. So, the unlimited liability partner is also expected to pay self-employment taxes.

ii. **Limited Liability Partnerships (LLPs):** On the other hand, every member of a limited liability partnership (LLP) is given limited liability as far as the partnership is concerned. This entails that an LPP protects each partner from debts owed in the name of the partnership entity (company). Similarly, the members won't be responsible for other partners' actions.

- **Limited Liability Company (LLC):** A limited liability company gives entrepreneurs the rare chance of combining the benefits of both the corporation and partnership types of business structures. This is because LLCs protect business owners from incurring personal liability on account of their companies. Your personal assets such as cars, homes, savings accounts, and others will not be liquidated to pay off debts in case your LLC fails or goes bankrupt.

With an LLC, it is possible to pass profits and losses through to the members' personal incomes. Hence, it is NOT mandatory for LLCs to pay corporation taxes in most U.S. States. Members of an LLC are considered to be self-employed and may be required to pay self-employment taxes and make appropriate contributions towards social security and Medicare.

Some U.S. States suggest a limited lifespan for their LLCs in the sense that when a member joins or leaves an LLC, it is required that the LLC be dissolved or re-established. The only way to get around this is if there has been an existing LLC agreement that clearly defines the procedures for buying, selling, or transferring company ownership to new owners.

- **Corporation:** Before LLCs became quite popular among entrepreneurs, most businesses were registered as corporations. There are five different types of corporations, each of them with its unique characteristics:

  i. **C Corp:** C Corporation offers the strongest protection for owners and shareholders. This means that the owner's personal assets are shielded from bankruptcy proceedings if the company suddenly collapses. However, it is more expensive to set up a corporation, and it is required, by Law, to pay taxes on its income as well as paying taxes through shareholders' personal tax returns when dividends are paid. C Corporate exists entirely as a separate entity from its founders and shareholders; shareholders can leave the company and sell their shares. This won't stop the corporation from operating as usual. Due to the complexity of its structure, corporations are expected to keep regular records of their processes, operations, and finances for proper accounting in accordance with company regulations of the State where the corporation is formed. Corporations can easily raise money from venture capitalists, banks, and other lenders.

  ii. **S Corp:** S Corporation (S Corp) is established to help entrepreneurs avoid the double taxation that C Corp is subjected to. In this way, profits and losses are passed directly to the owner's personal income and are taxed thus. The S Corp will not be subjected to a second corporation tax. It is advisable to ask for guidance while electing to have your corporation designated as an S

Corp. Some States do not recognize this designation and still double-tax the corporation as they would do to a C Corp.

iii. **B Corp:** B Corporation (a benefit corporation) is recognized by some U.S. States as the most appropriate legal business structure given to for-profit corporations. B Corp is different from C Corp in accountability, transparency, and purpose, but it is taxed as C Corp.

iv. **Close Corporation:** Close corporation is reportedly similar to B Corporation but it doesn't have an elaborate structure. It doesn't have a board of directors and is mostly managed by a handful of shareholders. Close corporations are barred from trading their shares publicly by some U.S. States.

v. **Nonprofit Corporation:** Often referred to as 501((3) corporations (which is a reference to the Internal Revenue Code that grants the corporation tax-exempt status), Nonprofit corporations are established to do charity in education, scientific work, religious, or literary activity. A nonprofit corporation is exempted from paying Federal and State taxes on its profits. However, it needs to strictly follow some organization rules that are similar to a C Corp's. Nonprofit corporations cannot distribute profits to members or political campaigns.

- **Cooperative:** A cooperative is a business owned by people who are using its services. When the business makes profits, they are shared among the owners of the business, which are also referred to as user-owners. A board of directors and officers are routinely elected to run the affairs of the cooperative, and each member is given a voting right. So, all members are equally given the opportunity to control the direction of the cooperative through their voting. A member may purchase as many shares of the cooperative as he/she wishes, but that doesn't translate into having more voting power over the other member-owners.

NOTE:
It is possible for an entrepreneur to combine the benefits of two or more types of companies. Take for instance, an LLC can elect to be taxed as a C Corp, S Corp, or even as a Nonprofit Organization.

3.2 Choosing the Best Company Type

If you are still wondering what is the best company type for the business you want to set up, the table below will help you make the best decision about which way to go:

Table 3.1 **Comparison of different legal business structures**

Business Structure	Ownership	Liability	Taxes
Sole Proprietorship	One person	Unlimited personal liability	Self-employment tax Personal tax
Partnership	Two or more people	Unlimited personal liability unless it is structured as a limited partnership	Self-employment tax (except for limited partners) Personal tax

Limited Liability Company (LLC)	One or more people	Owners are not personally liable	Self-employment tax Personal tax or corporate tax
Corporation-C Corp	One or more people	Owners are not personally liable	Corporate tax
Corporation-S Corp	One or more people, but no more than 100, all must be U.S. citizens	Owners are not personally liable	Personal tax
Corporation-B Corp	One or more people	Owners are not personally liable	Corporate tax
Corporation-Nonprofit	One or more people	Owners are not personally liable	Tax-exempt, but corporate profits can't be distributed

Source: Table 3.1 is obtained from Small Business Administration (SBA)

3.3 Company Registration and Other Necessary Documentation

Let's assume you have finally chosen a legal business structure/ company type and are proceeding to the next stage in your entrepreneurship journey—to actually register your company. There are some requirements that must be met before your business can be officially registered. Some of the essential steps to be taken are highlighted below:

1. **Choose a business name:** Every company has its unique name. This is good for differentiation; if your business' name is not peculiar or unique, consumers will confuse it with an existing business/company and you may have a hard time convincing them to trust your products/services. For example, there is a company in China that names its leather handbags, shoes, phone cases, and passport covers "IPHONE". Even though Apple, Inc. lost the trademark battle to the Chinese company, most people in America and Europe will not buy a product with a stolen trademark.

2. **Pick your business location:** When deciding on registering a business/company, location is the key. There are a lot of important issues to consider: Are you siting your company close to the sources of the required raw materials? Are your target customers living in the demographic/location you have selected? Is the cost of running a business in that location manageable and affordable? Is it easy to get licenses and other permissions in case you would need them down the line? Are the taxes reasonable? Will you be able to find qualified employees in that locality who will help you run your company?

3. **Register your business:** There are different avenues for registering a company, some of these approaches are discussed as follows:

   • **Federal agencies:** Even though it is not required that you register your business with the federal agencies, you will still need to take some actions if you need the following documentations: To get a federal tax ID (EIN), you will need to register with IRS; to obtain trademark or brand name for your company/product, you should get in touch with the United States Patent and Trademark Office; to get tax-exempt status for your nonprofit organization, you need to contact IRS; and, to establish an S Corp, you will be required to file Form 2553 with the IRS.

- **Local agencies:** You are not required to register your business with the county or city governments. However, you may need to apply for some licenses or permits to operate within a county or city.

- **State agencies:** Most companies in operation are registered with the respective State agencies. It is advisable that you register your business in the State where your primary business activities will be taking place. To avoid any legal loopholes, entrepreneurs may consider registering their companies in a State where any or all these activities take place. Most of your revenues are coming from the State; many of your employees are residing in the State; your company regularly has in-person meetings and events in the State. Over the years, the process of registering a company has been streamlined. You can register a new company online, by mail, or in person. Most U.S. States require that entrepreneurs register their new businesses with the Secretary of State, a Business Agency, or a Business Bureau.

Some of the required documents for State filing or registration of your company include:

- **Your business name**

- **Your business location**

- **Expected ownership, management structure, or the board of directors**

- Registered agent information

- Projected number and value of shares (if your company is a corporation)

- Other legally binding documents shown in Table 3.2 below

| Table 3.2 | List of required documents for registering a company (which varies from one U.S. State to another) |

Business structure	Document	Description
LLC	Articles of organization	Articles of organization is a simple document that describes the basics of your LLC. It includes business information like the company name, address, member names, and the registered agent.
LLC	LLC operating agreement	An operating agreement describes the structure of your company's financial and functional decisions. It defines how key business decisions are made, as well as each member's duties, powers, and responsibilities. It's widely recommended to create one to protect yourself and your business, even if your state doesn't mandate it.
Limited partnership	Certificate of limited partnership	This simple document describes the basics of your limited partnership. It notifies the state of the partnership's existence and contains basic business information like the company name, address, and partner names. Not all states require it, and some states call it by a different name

Limited partnership	Limited partnership agreement	A limited partnership agreement is an internally binding document between all partners that defines how business decisions get made, and each partner's duties, powers, and responsibilities. It's widely recommended to create one to protect yourself and your business, even if your state doesn't mandate it.
Limited liability partnership	Certificate of limited liability partnership	This simple document describes the basics of your limited liability partnership. It notifies the state of the partnership's existence and contains basic business information like the company name, address, and partner names. Not all states require it, and some states call it by a different name.
Limited liability partnership	Limited liability partnership agreement	A limited liability partnership agreement is an internally binding document between all partners that defines how business decisions get made, each partner's duties, powers, and responsibilities. It's widely recommended to create one to protect yourself and your business, even if your state doesn't mandate it.
Corporation (any kind)	Articles of incorporation	The articles of incorporation — or a certificate of incorporation — is a comprehensive legal document that lays out the basic outline of your business. It's required by every state when you incorporate. The most common information included is the company name, business purpose, number of shares offered, value of shares, directors, and officers.

| Corporation (any kind) | Bylaws or resolutions | By laws (called resolutions for nonprofits) are the internal governance documents of a corporation. They define how key business decisions are made, as well as officer and shareholders' duties, powers, and responsibilities. It's widely recommended to create one to protect yourself and your business, even if your state doesn't mandate it. |

Source: Table 3.2 is obtained from Small Business Administration (SBA)

NOTE:

Most State Agencies responsible for registering new companies/businesses prefer working with registered agents that are based within the State jurisdiction.

A registered agent helps you organize your company and acts as your representative to the Secretary of State. They obtain documents from the office on your behalf and submit to the same office on your company's behalf.

4. **Why file for foreign qualification?** If your company is located in New York State but carries out business operations in more than one state, it is advisable that you file for foreign qualification in those other States where your company is very active. Your company is mainly domestic in New York, but it is considered foreign in the other states where it has some presence.

Your company will then be required to pay taxes in all States where it is domestic and foreign. To qualify your business for foreign qualification in a State, you need to file a Certificate of Authority with the State. Some States may also ask you for a Certificate of Good Standing from your domestic State.

3.4 Welcome to Entrepreneurship: It's Time to Run Your Company

A company cannot run itself; it needs you — the entrepreneur to get up and manage it.

Not everyone can become an entrepreneur because of the amount of effort required to make it successful

Statistics (Fortunly)

- Only 78.5% of small businesses survive their first year.

- 29% of businesses fail because they run out of cash.

- The most common reason small businesses fail is that the market simply doesn't need their product or service.

So, don't feel SAD. SAD is the acronym for Sacrifice, Attention, and Demanding.

Sacrifice: You will be required to sacrifice everything you have to make your business succeed. This may include time, money, and every other resource at your disposal.

Attention: Your company will take almost 95 percent of your attention. You will have to squeeze time to do normal things with family, kids, and friends.

Demanding: Running a business is very demanding. There is no room for a slight error or else everything you have spent years building may come crashing down.

Do not be scared though, entrepreneurship is a joyful ride if you are careful, dedicated, and goal-oriented. It could also bring you large amounts of wealth if you are fortunate to strike gold, literally.

Quiz

1. **A Sole Proprietorship doesn't need to be officially registered by any agency.**

   a. False

   b. True

   c. I don't know.

2. **What kind of corporation can be used for charity and other nonprofit activities?**

   a. S Corp

   b. B Corp

   c. 501((3) corporation

3. **What does a registered agent do?**

   a. They do nothing

   b. They liaise between your company and the business registration agency in each state.

   c. I don't know.

4. **Which is NOT true about Limited Partnerships (LP)?**

   a. An LP has one general partner with unlimited liability

   b. The general partner mainly controls the partnership.

   c. All partners have the same unlimited liabilities.

5. **You are NOT required to register your company in one of these agencies.**

    a. State Business Bureau

    b. State Secretary of State

    c. Local agency like city and county governments

6. **According to Fortunly, what percentage of businesses survive their first year?**

    a. 20%

    b. 78.5%

    c. 10%

7. **What percentage of businesses fail for running out of cash?**

    a. 90%

    b. 29%

    c. 12%

8. **Why should a company file for foreign qualification?**

    a. When it conducts business activities in other States where it isn't domestic

    b. Because the owner doesn't understand the company laws

    c. When it wants to hire new employees

9. **The document that describes the basics of your Limited Liability Company (LL is called _____**

   a. Partnership agreement

   b. Articles of Organization

   c. Bylaws or resolutions

10. **What is unique about LLCs?**

   a. The owner has limited liability

   b. It is very cheap to set up

   c. It can be established in all U.S. States

Answers	1 – b	2 – c	3 – b	4 – c	5 – c
	6 – b	7 – b	8 – a	9 – b	10 – a

Chapter Summary

◆ The main types of legal business structures in most U.S. states are Sole Proprietorship, Partnerships, Limited Liability Companies (LLCs), Corporations, and Cooperatives.

◆ Entrepreneurs are expected to choose the business structure that fits the kind of business idea they are trying to actualize.

◆ Each company/business structure has specific ownership arrangements, taxes, and liabilities.

◆ Before a company can be registered by an entrepreneur, he/she needs to select a name, location, agree on ownership structure, management structure, number and value of shares, and present other legally required documents as shown in Table 3.3

◆ It may sometimes be cumbersome to do all the paperwork of registering a company by yourself. In this situation, it is advisable that you use the service of a Registered Agent who will liaise with the State business registration agency on your company's behalf.

References

- Fortunly (2022, January 18). Small business failure statistics to know in 2022—a realistic picture. Retrieved from www.fortunly.com

- U.S. Small Business Administration (SB (2022). Choose a business structure. Retrieved from www.sba.gov

This page is intentionally left blank

Chapter **4**

Your Products or Services or Both

A tangible object that is offered for purchase, consideration, or consumption is referred to as a product. A service is an immaterial good that results from the labor of one or more people. Services are typically intangible, whereas products are not always physical; they could be software or other digital products.

Every CEO and top executive fantasizes about running a successful corporation. Success depends on a compelling description of your product or service. A company has to be able to describe its products, services, and offerings in a compelling and unambiguous manner. Without that, there is no way a buyer can discover, comprehend, get attracted to, or buy what is being sold.

Key learning objectives should include the reader's understanding of the following

- Products/services offering
- Products/services solving consumer's problems

- Product/service pricing

- Product/service quality

- Product/service positioning in the marketplace

4.1 What Products/Services Will You be Offering to the World?

What will I sell? This should be one of the first concerns you must address when deciding to launch your own business. You probably already have some concepts of what you want to offer but may be finding it difficult to focus on how to package and present your goods or services to the potential customers.

It is advisable that aspiring entrepreneurs should focus their attention on niches or industries that are underserved. For instance, there is probably a lot of competition if you provide web development services, but if you specialize in handling web development services for dentists, you may stand out from the crowd.

More so, your product/service offering should be what your targeted customers want. No one is happy to spend their hard-earned money on things that will be useless to them. This is why it is emphasized that you should undertake prior research or investigation to determine exactly what you should offer to your prospective customers. This will save you time and resources.

There isn't any fast rule about this: Give people what they want and desire and then you are in business!

4.2 Will Your Products/Services Solve Some Problems Faced by Consumers?

You need to learn how to choose and provide the best products or services in a crowded market if you want to be a successful entrepreneur. Your capacity for decision-making will influence your success or failure more than any other thing.

Many of the products and services that people use now are not the same ones that they used five years ago. And many of the products that will be in use five years from now will be brand-new and different from what we have now.

Consumers have the unique opportunities to choose from countless products and services today. This offers you some chances to enter into the market and engage in profitable competition with a fresh product or service that outperforms those of your rivals. Keep in mind that your success will depend greatly on your ability to produce and market that product or service.

Thinking is the most crucial action you can take before choosing what to sell. Additionally, the more you consider a product or service before launching it, the better selection you'll make.

So where do you begin? You need to be personally and emotionally invested in a product's success in order to make it successful. Once you've decided on a product or service, you should start by conducting a self-analysis:

- *What kinds of goods do you prefer, value, use, and gain from?*

- *Do you like the product or service you intend to provide to your customers?*

- *Are you able to see yourself being enthusiastic about this product or service?*

- *Would you purchase it and utilize it if you are in your customers' position?*

- *Suppose the customers are your mother, best friend, or next-door neighbor; Would you sell your products to him/her/them?*

- *Can you imagine yourself continuing to market this product in the next five to ten years?*

- *Do you have a strong desire to introduce this product or service to the market?*

After that, consider the product or service from the perspective of the customer:

- *What will this product/service accomplish, prevent, or maintain for the consumer?*

- *In what ways does the product/service make your customers' lives or jobs better?*

- *Who are the target clients you'll be selling the product to?*

- *Will the customers who will be using this product or service personally fall in love with it?*

Assuming you have hired a management consultant to guide you about the introduction of this new product or service into the market, they're likely going to ask you these direct questions about the proposed product/service:

- *At your offering price, is there actually a market for the product?*

- *Is there enough demand for you to turn a profit?*

- *Is the demand sufficiently concentrated to allow for cost-effective marketing, sales, and delivery of the product?*

In addition to the questions above, you need to find some cogent answers to the following important questions that may help you make an informed decision about which product/ service to offer to your customers:

- *What exactly is being sold? Give a brief description of the product's benefits to the customer.*

- *Whom will the product be sold to? Specify who your ideal client is.*

- *What cost will you need to set the product at in order to make a profit?*

- *Who will be the product's salesperson?*

- *How will the product be marketed? What technique for marketing or sales will you employ?*

- *How will the goods or service be created or manufactured?*

- *Who is going to pay for the merchandise and how?*

- *What method will be used to deliver the goods or service to the customer?*

- *How will it be maintained, fixed, guaranteed, or replaced?*

Before you settle down on a service or product offering, there are a number of other inquiries you need to make.

- *Is there a genuine need for the product or service in the market right now?*

- *Is your new offering superior to what is already in the market?*

- *What three characteristics set your product apart from the competition?*

- *Is your product more affordable or of higher quality than everything else in the market?*

- *Do you believe you could dominate the market as the leading provider of this product or service?*

A product or a service must be the right one, sold to the appropriate buyer at the right time, in the right market, for it to be successful.

Don't make a product first and start looking for the problems it can solve!

Most individuals look for solutions rather than products while trying to solve their problems. You might be wasting your money and time if customers can't see how your solutions could help them address their difficulties. Additionally, if the issue you are attempting to tackle isn't interesting enough or lacking commercial capability, running a company will be extremely difficult.

Here's how to change your company's strategy so that the solution, not the product, is the main thing you focus on:

- **Sell the advantages rather than the thing**
  Selling effectively requires demonstrating to potential consumers how your offering will satisfy their demands and why it is the best choice. The merits of your product should be highlighted in the clearest possible terms.

  If they are unable to point out the benefits of purchasing your products, customers will probably switch to a different business that can help them. Prior to even introducing the product, your primary objective is to attract people's attention. Anyone who has ever chosen to buy a product does so because they have an issue bothering them. Find the issue, state the advantage, then describe how your solution will address it.

- **Features are wonderful, but they are not the goal**
  Each feature you incorporate into your product should provide a distinct benefit. Therefore, instead of listing several features, concentrate on the main reasons why the buyer will benefit from what you are offering.

- **Make sure your marketing message isn't solely focused on your product**
  Can you explain why people ought to pick your product above your rivals'? What makes you the best choice out there? Would you pay close attention to the marketing or sales communications you are adopting now if you were a potential customer? It may be challenging to convert leads into customers if your marketing message is inappropriate or misleading even if you have the best solution in the market.

  Start prioritizing your customers' expectations and concentrate on communicating with them through messaging that pointedly addresses their issues and explains how your solution can solve them.

4.3 Product/Service Pricing

There are three main approaches to pricing everything (product or service):

1. Pricing that is cost-based

2. Pricing that is dependent on the market

3. Pricing that is value-based

Pricing that is cost-based

A cost-based pricing is exactly what it sounds like; the cost of a good or service is calculated, and a standard margin is added to the cost. For instance, if a widget costs $2.50 to produce, a 50% basic margin would result in a $5.00 pricing for the widget.

Pricing dependent on the market

Market-based pricing, or pricing that is comparable to or close to your competition, refers to setting a product or service's price based on its market competitive position. For instance, as pricing is determined by what the marketplace is willing to pay, commodities (raw materials, agricultural products, essential materials, or mining products) frequently fall under this heading. Companies that change their prices to match the prices of the same products in the market are another common example of market-based pricing.

Pricing that is value-based

The final strategy is value-based pricing, which is typically the most challenging to implement. According to the buyer's perspective, this pricing method aims to assess the "value" of a product or service and then set a price dependent on that value.

The price of business-class airplane tickets is a classic illustration of value-based pricing. A certain group of consumers find business-class tickets to be very valuable since they provide more comfort, early boarding, meal service, and well-rested arrivals (which are particularly valuable on lengthy trips). As a result, airlines charge a premium for these tickets.

The Advantages and Disadvantages of the Three Strategies for Pricing

After reviewing the three most common pricing techniques, let's go into more detail about each one's advantages and disadvantages.

The advantages and disadvantages of cost-based pricing

The most common method of pricing is cost-based pricing since it is simple to compute, generally objective, generates predictable margins, and doesn't take a lot of work to implement.

Customers may easily justify cost-based pricing because it is such an easy way to think about price:

If it costs x to create the final product, the producer needs to make a profit by charging x plus a margin.

Cost-based/cost-plus pricing does have some significant disadvantages, though. The most obvious of these is that it is internally focused considering just internal cost problems and ignoring external forces like a customer's willingness to pay more.

The authenticity of the "cost" used to determine the pricing is another serious flaw. It might be challenging to link fixed costs to certain goods or services in a business. Changes in input costs result in various allocations of fixed expenses. There are numerous factors that might affect cost inside an organization, which can result in customers not believing that the production costs are accurate and avoiding buying the product. Inaccurate cost estimates could prevent reaching the desired standard margin.

The advantages and disadvantages of market-based pricing

Market-based pricing looks toward external market conditions to determine prices rather than being internally focused like cost-based pricing.

The commodity market is where market-based pricing is most frequently used. The truth is that market-based pricing is the most common type of pricing for those industries that are not commodity-based, such as the service industry. Pricing based on important competitors occurs when businesses compare their prices to those of their main rivals, who may be industry leaders or rivals in terms of both size and location.

For example, in the culinary services sector, vendors providing restaurant raw ingredients must consider the market pricing. Restaurants frequently choose the least expensive ingredient because it is just a component of the dish and will do everything to avoid wasting money on ingredients when there are others offering the same ingredients for cheaper prices in the market. It is especially advantageous for businesses with a cost advantage in the market.

Market-based pricing does, however, have disadvantages. The market-based strategy, like cost-plus pricing, does not take the buyer's desire to pay into account, which means money could be lost.

It is also important to note that it can be challenging and unreliable to obtain competitive market information in certain businesses, making it challenging to set pricing that is comparable to those of your rivals. The significant competitive price is tracked by several services, however, because prices are combined to preserve privacy, these are frequently expensive and unreliable.

When contrasted to cost-plus pricing, market-based pricing offers a better appearance, but it still ignores the buyer or customer's input and, thus, the opportunity for more profit.

The advantages and disadvantages of value-based pricing

When determining the price of a product or service, value-based pricing advances the approach for pricing strategy by taking the customer's willingness to pay into account.

Although it has gained popularity over several years, this strategy also ranks among the most challenging to implement. This strategy is used by marketing teams because it measures and rewards the worth a service or product provides.

It is well-known because it is possible to maximize revenue by giving clients as much value as possible by charging precisely what they are ready to pay. However, one needs to be able to estimate the perceived quality and, consequently, the customer's willingness to pay in order to set prices based on value.

The problem is that while these operations call for specialized knowledge and time, the majority of businesses lack the internal resources to carry them out. Value-based pricing is not only more expensive than the other two pricing systems, but it is also more difficult to implement. After all, the willingness of different clients to pay varies.

Value-based pricing relies on segmentation, which involves knowing what types of customer groups exist and what those groups' individual perceptions of value are in relation to others.

4.4 Product/Service Quality

Customer satisfaction results from services and products that meet or surpass their expectations. A customer weighs the value of the product or service against the amount of money they are about to exchange before making a purchase.

The operational or manufacturing value or quality of products and services is expressed in the sense that they are manufactured to standards which are reflected in their overall market prices.

Irrespective of how operations see quality, the customer's perspective always contrasts what they want with what they get. How do consumers come to have certain expectations?

Quality, however, depends on the customer's perception of the product or service they have received.

When we discuss a product or service's quality, we want to discover how well it meets a demand or expectation. Does it have each of the qualities we're looking for? If so, we can conclude that the goods or services are of very high quality. Even if it has a slight flaw, we could still consider it to be of high quality. It qualifies as poor quality if it significantly falls short of our expectations. We would deem it to be of unsatisfactory quality if it were absolutely useless. This eliminates the notion that a service or product is either of high quality or not. All of us desire perfection, yet it is neither feasible nor economical.

4.5 Product/Service Positioning in the Marketplace

The process of establishing a new product's position in a consumers' eyes is known as product positioning. It involves examining the market and the positions of the competitors, determining where a new product stands in comparison to the competition, and promoting the product image of a specific brand.

Companies can use product positioning to make their products stand out and be known by employing channels of communication, pricing, or product quality.

What makes product positioning crucial?

To create a product that speaks to their requirements, brands must get to know their customers. A well-planned strategy can pinpoint this product's position in the market and its advantages for customers.

Businesses might base their positioning on one of these five major tactics:

1. **Positioning depending on features of the product**

   When you use a product's features or benefits as part of your positioning strategy, your brand is linked to a specific benefit that people will appreciate.

   Consumers are continuously informed by brands of a special feature or benefit of the product.

2. **Price-based positioning**

   Pricing that is competitive means it focuses on the cost of products or services. A brand typically pursues being the cheapest or the lowest in the market using a pricing positioning plan, and value determines its stance.

   Price-sensitive customers will frequently buy them even without knowing the cost because they know it is frequently the lowest alternative because of their lower logistics and distribution costs.

3. **Choosing a position based on luxury or quality**

   In the consumer's opinion, a product's price and quality are frequently in line because a high price is frequently linked with a high level of quality. Placing a product according to its high caliber or "luxury" is distinct from positioning a product according to price.

   These businesses fail to mention their price point; rather, they emphasize their high quality in order to spark consumers' interest and make them buy the product irrespective of its cost.

4. **Positioning based on the application or use of the product**
   An additional strategy for positioning your brand in the marketplace is to link your product with a certain application.

   For example, for anyone who needs a quick, simple meal on the road but lacks time, meal replacement supplements can be helpful.

   There are also meal substitutes that are specifically made for athletes or those who wish to do well in the gym, thus they frequently have extra vitamins and minerals and are heavy in calories.

5. **Choosing a position based on the opposition**
   Utilizing the competitors as a point of comparison for differentiation is the focus of competitor-based positioning.

   In order to make their product or service stand out from competing options on the market, brands emphasize a crucial distinction that their product or service delivers.

   Brands should possess a point of differentiation and emphasize it in their communication. Without one, you merge into the background of the market. Give customers a memorable experience!

Quiz

1. A tangible object that is offered for purchase is called _____

   a. Services

   b. Product

   c. Matter

2. What is the most crucial action you can take before choosing what to sell?

   a. Thinking

   b. Worrying

   c. Crying

3. Which one is not the main approach to product pricing?

   a. Pricing that is Cost-based

   b. Pricing that is Customer-based

   c. Pricing that is Value-based

4. Quality depends on the customer's _____

   a. money

   b. perception

   c. wants

5. **Your capacity for decision-making will influence your success or failure more than any other aspect**

   a. Yes

   b. No

   c. Not sure

6. **Before settling for a novel product, which is not part of the inquiries you need to make?**

   a. Is your new offering superior to what is already on the market?

   b. How do I make money?

   c. Is your new offering inferior to what is already on the market?

7. **If the issue you are attempting to tackle isn't interesting enough, running a firm will be _____**

   a. easy

   b. difficult

   c. normal

8. **Before introducing the product, your primary objective is to attract _____.**

   a. people's attention.

   b. money

   c. awards

9. It may be challenging to convert leads into customers if your marketing message is inappropriate or misleading even if you have the best solution in the market.

   a. Never

   b. Yes

   c. Sometimes

10. Pricing that is comparable to or close to your competition is called _____

    a. market-based pricing

    b. cost-based pricing

    c. customer-based pricing

Answers	1 – b	2 – a	3 – b	4 – b	5 – a
	6 – b	7 – b	8 – a	9 – b	10 – a

Chapter Summary

◆ Quality depends on the customer's perception of the good or service they have received.

◆ It is not advisable to make a product first and then look for problems it can solve.

◆ Businesses continue to price their products/services using value-based, cost-based, or market-dependent pricing method.

◆ Irrespective of how operations see quality, the customer's perspective always contrasts what they want with what they get.

◆ Your brand's positioning in the marketplace establishes where it stands in relation to rival brands and offers it a distinctive character.

References

- Tracy, Brian (2005, July 18). Choosing a Product or Service to Sell. Entrepreneur.com. Retrieved from www.entrepreneur.com

- Transition Support (2022, August 22). What is product quality and how is it determined? Retrieved from www.transition-support.com

Chapter **5**

What It Takes to Successfully Manage a Company

In the words of Richard Branson - "If you can run one business well, you can run any business well." Any business, whether small, micro, large, or online, requires proper management of human resources, time, finance and/or money, modern technology, fresh and innovative ideas, and cooperation, among other things. Always keep in mind that the customer is king in any business. An efficient entrepreneur not only draws in new customers but also retains his present ones in order to maximize profits by providing the best products and services in line with his customers' existing needs and requirements.

As a result, running a business doesn't only mean creating products and services, selling them for money, and making profits. Since there are a lot of risks involved, a business person must be adaptable and dynamic to adjust to and making profits. Since there are a lot of risks involved, a businessperson must be adaptable and dynamic to adjust to shifting customer demands and needs as a result of their new experiences every day while keeping in mind the most crucial factor: "Providing the customers with the finest service or product and after-service at an affordable price which keeps the customers as well as ends up making good profits, makes it a win-win scenario for the business."

Key learning objectives should include the reader's understanding of the following

- Business planning

- Eliminating self-limiting beliefs

- Failure is-not-an-option mentality

- The place of luck in entrepreneurial success

Let's take a look at how to manage a business effectively: Before you can successfully direct the affairs of your company, you must pay attention to the following processes:

Effective communication

The foundation of any business is communication. The best outcomes can only be achieved through effective communication, whether you are talking with your employees, customers, or partners. The most efficient method of communication is face-to-face because it makes the message clear and instills a sense of trust and accountability.

The process of communication is two-way. Everyone should be on the same page when debating the plan and assigning duties, so that nothing is changed and everyone has the same understanding of the plan and how it will be carried out.

A prompt brainstorming

Getting ideas from each person in a company is part of the brainstorming process. In a hierarchical structure, this is done at various stages in the form of micro teams, and then final suggestions are conveyed to the senior management for approval. Additionally, in smaller companies, the owner can call a meeting with every employee to solicit input on a particular issue.

The nicest thing about brainstorming is that it allows you to express yourself freely without the fear of criticism or accusation, provided, of course, that your ideas are guarded by logic. This results in all employees (whether they are seasoned pros or up-and-coming talent) contributing new, creative ideas as a result of feeling more confident and being a part of the team.

Effectual planning

The art of planning is forward-looking and goal focused. It is crucial for an entrepreneur to have at least two to three functional plans (Plan A, B, and in place so that if one fails or he/she needs to adjust his course of action, he/she is prepared with a backup strategy that will yield the greatest possible outcomes.

Planning well and consistently implementing it are the surest ways to successfully manage a company. Planning brings clarity and will make running a company simple for you. You must first of all hammer out a solid plan that should consider both the favorable and unfavorable situations that can have effects on your business.

5.1 Business Planning

An extensive written document known as a business plan outlines the objectives and goals of a company. A business plan explains all the applicable strategies that have been documented for carrying out the operations, financing, and marketing of the organization. Both new and existing businesses need business plans.

A business plan is an important document that is written for both external and internal audiences. For instance, a good business plan can be used to attract funding before a company has established a proven track record. That's a typical example of an external audience.

Concerning the internal audience, the executive team of a company can utilize a business plan to highlight important actions that should be taken and outline the procedures for meeting scheduled goals. A business plan can be broadly classified into four different forms: They are the very brief plans, also known as mini plans, presentation plans, working plans, and what-if plans. Each of these business plans can be used in different circumstances, as described below.

The Mini Plan

The Mini Plans are the easiest to prepare and they are mostly used by "moms and pops"—which are small businesses owned by individuals.

The requirements in mini plans are the same as in any other type of business plans, but they are not specifically elaborated on.

The Presentation Plan

The Presentation Plan, otherwise known as the "Pitch Deck" is primarily used to pitch businesses or companies to possible partners or investors. This kind of business plan has all the business plan's requirements but they mostly address the kind of information that would be interesting to potential partners or investors.

The Working Plan

When people talk about the traditional business plans, they are actually referring to the "working plan". This type of business plan contains detailed step-by-step procedures required to smoothly run a company. It presents adequate information about a company's mission and vision, financials, marketing strategy, organizational or management approaches, and market analysis.

The What-If Plan

When faced with unforeseen circumstances, you need to modify your business's operational strategy. You might want to prepare a backup plan that will help your business survive an emergency such as unexpected crises, natural disasters, etc. What-if plans, also known as contingency plans, are strategic plans based on one of the worst-case scenarios you can ever imagine happening to your business, such as losing market share, dealing with fierce price rivalry, or having a key CEO quit the organization. A contingency plan could ease creditors' or investor's fear by demonstrating that you have made adequate preparations to weather any unforeseen disasters.

Sample Business Plan

A Sample Business Plan for a Small Service Business

You can use this sample business plan for a small service business to guide you in designing your own. The information provided here demonstrates how best to prepare your business plan as a service provider. So, you will be required to supply exact information about your own business in the plan.

Executive Summary

Sanders Infotech is a Software as a Service (SaaS) business that provides enterprise solutions for small- and mid-sized companies. Sanders offers a suite of Customer Relationship Management (CRM) software services that will help enterprises maintain good relationships with their customers.

Based in Nashville, Tennessee, Sanders Infotech combines exquisite frontend designs with the latest SaaS technologies to facilitate the procedures adopted by companies for obtaining, processing, storing, and retrieving their customers' data that could be used in making informed, company-wide customer service decisions.

Customers can subscribe to this service while utilizing Sanders' affordable cloud technology.

Company Overview

Sanders Infotech is a Limited Liability Company (LL that is founded by two people, Mr. King James and Ms. Diana George, who owns fifty percent of the company each.

From Nashville, Tennessee, Sanders is established to primarily help businesses manage their CRM systems. Good customer service is very essential for increasing revenue and achieving a high profitability rate. Unfortunately, not all companies have a great CRM process in place, and Sanders infotech is born to help them bridge the gap in their CRM systems.

Business Description (Service Description)

Customers can subscribe to the three types of Customer Relationship Management services offered by Sanders Infotech, namely CRM 1, CRM2, and CRM 3. Monthly and annual subscriptions are possible.

CRM 1: This system is deployed to help companies obtain vital data from their customers. It also has in-built data processing, storing, and retrieval features. Businesses can measure the responsiveness of their customers to their customer service activities and see if certain desirable metrics are met.

CRM 2: This is a telephony/communication software that streamlines the communication and interaction between businesses and their many customers. This tool can be customized based on the company's size and requirements.

CRM 3: This is an accounting tool that tries to match CRM efficiency with revenue generation. There are some metrics in the software that helps businesses identify if their better customer service is leading to more sales, revenues, and of course, higher profitability.

The entire CRM architecture is managed by experienced front-end and back-end programmers and data scientists who will work closely with each business in customizing the much-needed CRM tools.

Customer Service Management software is always in high demand as companies explore ways to increase sales and actualize their profitability expectations.

Market Analysis

Sanders infotech will target small- and medium-sized companies that aim to improve their customer service management procedures. The expected customers cut across all industries, and their locations are immaterial. In other words, Sanders Infotech will be providing CRM services globally.

SWOT Analysis: The strength of Sanders Infotech lies in its capacity to serve businesses having different sizes. More importantly, the technologies developed by Sanders are proprietary and have been patented or trademarked.

One major weakness Sanders Infotech possesses is that it has to compete with other CRM companies that are already in the marketplace.

Sanders can explore the opportunities in emerging economies or third-world countries that have companies that seriously need its proprietary technologies.

The major threat against the wide application of Sanders Infotech CRM technologies is that it is currently in English. This means that it cannot be localized to other languages at the moment, but Sanders will work on achieving that in the next 5 years.

Operating Plan

It is expected that well-trained, in-house tech professionals comprising experienced software and software engineers and data scientists will oversee the day-to-day operations of Sanders Infotech. More importantly, the professionals have had hands-on (practical) experiences in the Customer Service departments of other companies before joining Sanders Infotech.

Customers will be able to pay for the CRM solutions offered digitally and through bank transfers.

Sanders' business operations will be managed at its physical office located in Nashville, Tennessee, but there is a plan to also hire some outsourced professionals or resources when necessary.

CRM 1, CRM 2, and CRM 3 are cloud-based and customers can operate entirely in the cloud. They are not expected to own any hardware; they are only required to download Sanders Infotech's apps (both windows and mobile).

Marketing and Sales Plan

All marketing avenues will be explored to promote Sanders' CRM solutions, including both traditional and digital marketing channels.

The key message to customers will be: "Make your customers happy, increase your revenue."

It may be necessary to attend tech expositions, conferences, and trade shows to showcase the usefulness of Sanders Infotech services.

Financial Plan

Sanders Infotech will raise the initial capital for its business activities and hope to increase its revenue year-on-year for the first 3 years of operating. Customers will be able to pay monthly, quarterly, or annually for the services they enjoy from Sanders infotech.

The profits for the first 5 years will be reinvested in the business until Sanders files for an IPO.

Income Statement for a sample fiscal year ending December 31, 20XX

Revenue: $5 million

Total Expenses: $1 million

Net Income Before Taxes: $4 million

Statement of Financial Position as of December 31, 20XX

Cash and Cash Equivalents: $2 million

Receivables: $1 million

Property and Equipment: $2 million

Intangible Assets: $500,000

Total Assets: $5.5 million

Balance Statement

The board of directors is expected to approve the 20XX fiscal year budget for Sanders Infotech which is estimated at $5 million in revenues and $1 million in expenditures. This reveals that the organization is profitable at the end of the fiscal year.

Cash Flow Statement for the Fiscal Year Ending December 31, 20XX

Operating Activities: Income Before Taxes –$500,000

Investing Activities: New equipment and supplies –$500,000

Raised capital = $5 million

Net Change in Cash: $4 million

According to the 20XX fiscal year financial statements for Sanders Infotech, the business' investments are projected to decrease by 5 percent, and it is projected to generate $5 million in revenues. Its total assets are valued at $5.5 million.

Appendix

This is where all other documents necessary for running Sanders Infotech will be placed.

Suggested reading:

For better understanding of the possible uses of business plans and how to make your own business plan, read "Business Plan Essentials" by Vibrant Publishers (ISBN - 9781636511214)

Sticking to Your Business Plan

If you follow a business plan, your company has a better chance of prospering. However, it's not always easy to do so. The suggestions below will help you stick to the business plan you have spent countless hours preparing:

1. **Review your business plan at regular intervals**

   Don't just glance over it. Spend some time reading your company strategy from beginning to the end. You will constantly be able to remind yourself about the primary reason for writing the plan, and starting the business, in the first instance and learn to stick to your goals.

2. **Know that all "plans" should be flexible**

   The best plans, both for business and otherwise, are somewhat flexible. This gives you the chance to regularly update your business approaches or strategies. As times change and business requirements expand, you will be able to finetune your business processes to meet up with the challenges from the new dispensations.

3. **Use your projections to help make financial decisions**

   When you first draft your company's business plan, you might depend mainly on projected figures to determine your possible expenses and profitability. However, as you start to run the actual business, it is imperative that you update your finances with real-time data that will show your business's true financial standing.

4. **Ask the professionals**

   If you are ever at a loss about how to update and refine your business plan from time to time, you should seek help from some financial professionals who can assist you in doing that. Some business development experts are knowledgeable in updating and expanding the scopes of business plans

5. **Use your business plan to set concrete goals**

   You can set measurable future goals with the help of your business plan. All you need to do is to use your updated business plan to estimate what the future looks like for your company.

5.2 Eliminating Self-Limiting Beliefs

Have you ever entertained any of these self-limiting statements?

"I'm not confident enough to run a business."

"I can't take any risks."

"This has probably already been done by someone else."

"My relatives and friends won't support my ambition to become an entrepreneur."

Surprisingly enough, your ability to accomplish your personal and professional goals may be limited by self-limiting beliefs. So let's start by examining what self-limiting beliefs are and how you can overcome them.

What are Typical Self-Limiting Beliefs?

Simply expressed, self-limiting beliefs are presumptions or assumptions you have about who you are and how the world sees you. These presumptions are "self-limiting" since they are preventing you from realizing your potential in some way.

Examples of Self-Limiting Business Beliefs include:

"I'm not qualified or possess sufficient experience."

This limiting notion is quite prevalent among would-be entrepreneurs. We frequently think that before we can take an action in our business or in other pursuits, we need a lengthy resume that is packed with decades of practical experiences.

"Probably someone else could do it better than me"

Have you ever considered a business concept but abandoned it because you assumed someone else had already executed it or could do it more effectively?

"I'm short of funds."

Of course, a genuine obstacle in entrepreneurship is lack of adequate funding. However, there are many ways to finance or bootstrap a company without spending a lot of money.

How to Overcome Your Self-Limiting Beliefs

Naturally, you want to dispel your limiting beliefs after they have occupied your mind. However, this is not an easy undertaking. Let's look at six methods that might be useful:

1. **Recognize their objectives**
    This may sound quite odd but try to investigate the notion behind those negative beliefs. What use could these false beliefs which are preventing you from moving forward in your business possibly serve? There may be some warnings or even an eye-opening experience.

2. **Interrogate them**

   Start to doubt if your belief is still true or helpful once you've determined its goal and where it comes from. Taking the step to directly challenge your limiting ideas might help lessen their overall influence on you.

3. **Make fun of them**

   Humor may be a powerful technique for unblocking negative self-talk. When you're laughing at something, it's difficult for it to have any powerful effect on you.

4. **Create brand-new Beliefs**

   You must also adopt new beliefs in order to erase the impact of your self-limiting ones. You can do this by creating a new belief that is more in line with your values and personal philosophy.

5. **Retrain your brain**

   Since beliefs are essentially sequences that the human subconscious recognizes, you may begin to rewire it by giving your brain new patterns of thoughts.

   Positive affirmations and meditation may help you rewire your brain.

5.3 Failure-Is-Not-An-Option Mentality

In business circles, one of the common mantras is that "failure is not an option". This places a lot of pressure on entrepreneurs and business executives to perform better than their rivals.

Luckily , science has shown that failures are fuel for better inventions. All the gadgets we are using today went through several iterations before the final, great products were made. If we apply this to business, when an entrepreneur fails in one venture, he/she can use the experiences garnered from that failure to establish a new business and drive it to outstanding success. There is a word for that in business parlance: Pivoting

Jack Ma, one of the founders of the Chinese e-commerce giant, Alibaba, once said, *"never give up. Today is hard, tomorrow will be worse, but the day after tomorrow will be sunshine. If you don't give up, you still have a chance. Giving up is the greatest failure."*

Instead of running away from failure or being afraid of embracing it, entrepreneurs should use failure as a stepping-stone to a greater business achievement.

5.4 Understanding the Place of Luck in Entrepreneurial Success

Entrepreneurs have come to the realization that there is no assurance of success in business. The experience of running a business demonstrates that, despite the best preparations and research, unpredictable, volatile turns of fate can either propel your firm to a greater level or, more readily, knock it to its knees.

They positioned themselves for success by working hard, remaining steadfast, and being determined. They are aware that doing business carries dangers. So whether or not they think luck plays a role in tipping the scales in one direction or the other, we think there are steps you can take to get ready for when luck, whether good or bad, shows up.

These are conditions that could turn a hardworking entrepreneur into an overnight lucky "person":

Timing

Successful business people are those who have a solid understanding of upcoming possibilities and trends. However, when great efforts meet the right timing, it can lead to an unimaginable entrepreneurial success. Several centuries ago, no one knew that something called the "internet" will revolutionize every aspect of human lifestyle, from education to commerce. Today, we all enjoy the amazing benefits of the internet that our forefathers were not fortunate to have in their times.

Openness to ideas

Many entrepreneurs develop their concepts almost by accident. Business owners frequently see ideas in almost everything and draw motivation from even the most routine tasks. Many business owners then experience a moment of clarity and find a method to enhance an existing good, service, or enterprise.

A strong support network

Starting a business is extremely stressful, but the greatest strategy for addressing and resolving problems is to have a strong support system. Your excitement for your company can be cultivated and encouraged by interacting with like-minded people such as business associates, partners, or mentors.

Quiz

1. Customer is king in any business.

    a. Yes

    b. No

    c. Sometimes

2. An efficient businessperson does all of these except_____

    a. drawing in new customers

    b. retaining current customers.

    c. reducing profits

3. One unsatisfied customer _____

    a. might turn away many more customers.

    b. can bring in more customers

    c. will not affect business.

4. The interdepartmental requirement that supports teamwork in any business is _____

    a. profit

    b. communication

    c. product

5. **Getting ideas from each person in a company is called**_____

    a. brain draining

    b. brainstorming

    c. brain shifting

6. **The best method to manage a company successfully is by**

    _____

    a. allowing chance

    b. planning well

    c. just funding

7. **Which is not a way of adhering to your business strategy?**

    a. Reviewing your business plan at regular intervals

    b. Neglecting the professionals

    c. Using your projections to help make financial decisions

8. **Your ability to accomplish your personal and professional goals may be affected by**_____

    a. positive declarations

    b. self-limiting beliefs

    c. strong values

9. **Which is not a way to overcome your self-limiting beliefs?**

   a. Making fun of them

   b. Interrogating and challenging them

   c. Accepting them

10. **Is "failure-is-not-an-option" mentality good?**

    a. No, it is stressful to entrepreneurs

    b. Yes, it forces companies to make only perfect products

    c. Never

Answers	1 – a	2 – c	3 – a	4 – b	5 – b
	6 – b	7 – b	8 – b	9 – c	10 – a

Chapter Summary

◆ Running a company doesn't only mean creating products and services, or selling them for money, and making profits, you must have a business plan and actually adhere to your business strategy.

◆ Your ability to accomplish your personal and professional goals may be limited by self-limiting beliefs. So begin to examine and tackle those beliefs that can hinder your progress.

◆ The old saying "the harder you work, the luckier you become" is definitely true.

◆ There are different types of business plans, such as mini plans, presentation plans (pitch decks), working plans, and what-if (contingency) plans.

◆ Communication in business is a tool that could enhance employees' brainstorming process and increase quality and value in the products/services they produce.

References

- Accion Opportunity Fund (2022, January 5). 5 Tips for Sticking to Your Business Plan. Retrieved from www.aofund.org

- Monica Krish (2011, December 11). Latest Business Plan – My Business World." My Business World. Retrieved from www.monicakrish.wordpress.com

Chapter **6**

Markets and Customers

The global economies have expanded significantly from the previous decades and organizations have identified some consumers' needs and are working round the clock to serve those markets.

Irrespective of the industry or size of the organization, every company does marketing to reach out to prospective customers that may be interested in their products/services. Thus market analysis and marketing go hand-in-hand.

Key learning objectives should include the reader's understanding of the following

- Market Segmentation

- What do customers want and how best to target them

- Meeting customers' expectations and winning their loyalty

6.1 Market Segmentation

You've invested time and resources into developing the ideal marketing plan, and you desire your message to be well received by your prospective customers, right?

As your audience grows, it becomes much easier for a message to get buried, misunderstood, or ignored entirely. Communication is an art. Your marketing message runs the risk of being meaningless to the majority of the people you're trying to reach as your audience gets bigger and their preferences, requirements, and opinions get more varied.

This is precisely why it's so important to classify your target markets. This method enables you to concentrate your sales efforts solely on distinct customer segments in order to better meet their unique demands and needs. By demonstrating to prospective consumers that you comprehend them and understand what they need best, you can provide your brand an edge over that of your rivals.

Some interesting statistics and fact (Statista)

- Number of social network users in the U.S (327.22 million)

- Social media ad spend in the U.S (80.7 billion USD)

- Leading social network platform used by marketers worldwide (Facebook)

What is Market Segmentation?

Market segmentation is a strategy used by brands to focus their marketing, promotion, and sales activities by breaking down their target audience into more manageable, smaller groups of people. Simply put, each market segment's customer shares traits that can be used by companies to their advantage.

Market segmentation is done to introduce a message that will be effectively received by everyone in that market segment. This is useful for businesses that might offer a product or service with numerous uses or advantages for various types of consumers.

Recognize that you can't satisfy everyone's needs and that as a business owner, you can't appeal to or solve everyone's problems. Market segmentation is a particularly successful growth strategy because of this very reason.

There are three different segmentation levels:

- **Strategic segmentation**
  This is to comprehend your company's market environment. Strategic segmentation aims to provide answers to queries like how do we grow? Which regions should we target? Which are the main market segments we serve?

- **Tactical segmentation**
  Determining the demands and drivers of your customers is one of the tactical segmentation's common goals. Recognize the features of the important portions. This segmentation aims to answer issues like: How can we stand out in the market categories that are of the utmost importance? What do we provide to different customer groups?

- **Operational segmentation**
  Identifying market segments based on resources, time, and value forms the foundation of operational segmentation. Operational segmentation can provide information on the following queries: Who are the customers we value the most? Whom do we offer special rates and advantages to?

Common mistakes in market segmentation

Here are some common mistakes entrepreneurs can commit when segmenting their targeted market for the first time. They include:

- Attempting to adopt a single segmentation model for various purposes.

- Segmenting information that does not cover all segments of the customer base..

- Using a variety of segmentation models, but finding no obvious or reliable connection between them.

- Not updating techniques as the customer base evolves resulting in false segmentation.

6.2 What Do Your Customers Want and How Best to Target Them?

No matter how great your service or product is, the basic fact is that if a person doesn't want it or feels they don't need it, they won't buy it. And unless you have a clear understanding of what your consumers' true needs are, you won't be able to convince anybody that they need to or desire to purchase what you're offering.

Every successful company, whether it sells products directly to consumers or to other enterprises, is built around knowing and comprehending the needs of the customer. Once you are aware of this, you can utilize it to convince both current and new customers that doing business with your company is to their greatest advantage.

This explains what you must know about your customers, how to apply this knowledge to market to them more successfully, and how to defeat your competition.

Ten things you should understand about your potential customers

1. **Who they are**
    Find out your consumers' demographics like gender, age, marital status, and occupation if you sell to individuals directly.

2. **What they do**
    If you sell to people directly, it's important to be aware of their professions and hobbies. It helps to know what your consumers are trying to accomplish if you are selling to them.

3. **Why they buy**
    Knowing why clients purchase a good or service makes it simpler to match their requirements with the advantages your company can provide.

4. **When they purchase**

   Your chances of achieving success will significantly rise if you engage a consumer right when they are ready to make a purchase.

5. **How they buy**

   For instance, some customers prefer to make purchases online, while others prefer in-person interactions. Recognizing how your target consumers prefer to make purchases will help you reach them at the right time and right place.

6. **How much do they possess?**

   If you can correlate what you're giving to what you believe your customer can afford, you'll have more success.

7. **What motivates them to make purchases?**

   Knowing what makes someone tick will enable you to provide for them in their preferred manner.

8. **Their expectations of you**

   For instance, you may see an increase in repeat business if your consumers depend on you for timely deliveries and you meet their expectations.

9. **What they believe about you**

   If the customers enjoy doing business with you, they'll probably buy more from you.

10. **What they believe about your rivals**

    You have a far higher likelihood of staying above your rivals if you are aware of how your customers feel about your competitors.

    In order to accomplish your primary business objectives, you must have a thorough grasp of your customers. Whether you wish to increase sales, create more engaging content, or enhance customer experience, knowing your customers better than they do is the key to success.

6.3 Meeting Customers' Expectations and Winning Their Loyalty

How to meet the needs of customers

It's time to examine your data once you've gathered all the information you require. Concentrate on using the knowledge obtained from the data to serve your consumers satisfactorily. You might need to assign a small group of individuals or the entire staff to this, depending on how much of a gap there is between your existing services and your results. In any case, to ensure that the procedure goes well, you should adhere to these four steps:

- **Identify** — pinpoint the requirements of your clients/customers.

- **Distribute** — Make the findings of your research available to your company's pertinent departments and stakeholders.

- **Create** — make a new item or launch a new service in response to the requirements and preferences of your target market.

- **Collect** — gather feedback on how well your new product matches your clients/customer's needs and how it performs. Then, go forward and use the information in servicing your customers better.

A satisfied customer is a customer who will always pay!

Keeping your customers satisfied and happy is crucial to the success of your company and figuring out their needs and desires is the first step in that direction! So keep in mind to go gradually. Start by determining their needs, the specific needs you want to address, as well as other aspects like their spending patterns, where and why they purchase, and the customer demographics. After that, you may concentrate your efforts on fulfilling their wants by designing items that are in line with your study findings!

Quiz

1. **The global economy has not expanded significantly from the previous decades.**

   a. Wrong

   b. Correct

   c. Only a bit

2. **It is crucial for marketers to consider the value of their targeted customer base before creating a product.**

   a. No

   b. Yes

   c. Not every time

3. **Which is not part of the goal of marketing?**

   a. Creating

   b. Delivering

   c. Consuming

4. **As the audience grows, it becomes much easier for a message to get misunderstood.**

   a. Correct

   b. Wrong

   c. Not always

5. **Communication is an art.**

   a. Yes

   b. No

   c. Maybe

6. **Market segmentation enables you to _____**

   a. distract sales efforts

   b. concentrate sales efforts

   c. mix sales efforts

7. **Demonstrating to prospective consumers that you comprehend them and understand what they need best can provide your brand with _____**

   a. an edge

   b. a slow sales

   c. an equal ground

8. **Market segmentation is done to introduce a message that will be well _____**

   a. neglected

   b. received

   c. of no effect

9. **Determining the demands of customers is one of the segmentation's common goals.**

   a. Yes

   b. No

   c. Maybe

10. **"Who are the customers we value the most?" is part of which segmentation?**

   a. Operational segmentation

   b. Strategic segmentation

   c. Tactical segmentation

Answers	1 – a	2 – b	3 – c	4 – a	5 – a
	6 – b	7 – a	8 – b	9 – a	10 – a

Chapter Summary

◆ Market segmentation enables you to concentrate your sales efforts on distinct customer segments in order to better meet their unique demands and needs.

◆ No matter how great your service or product is, the basic fact is that if a person doesn't want it or feels they don't need it, they won't buy it.

◆ Keeping your customers satisfied is crucial for the success of your company and figuring out their needs and desires is the first step in that direction!

◆ Market segmentation is one of the greatest weapons an entrepreneur has for maximizing the use of resources while discovering how exactly to make his/her customers happy and satisfied.

◆ Marketing involves targeting people with the products/ services that they need and hope will help them solve some pain points.

References

- Stanimirovic, Uros (2021, February 2). The Ultimate Guide on How to Identify Customer Needs and Wants. Retrieved from www.brid.tv

- Info Entrepreneurs (2022, August 17). Know your customers' needs. Retrieved from www.infoentrepreneurs.org

This page is intentionally left blank

Chapter **7**

Handling Your Competitors

To be a successful brand in business, you need to find ways to stay ahead of the competition. Be aware that someone somewhere is either nurturing the same business idea as you are or is already starting the business. Therefore, market competition is really hard and there are no easy answers to winning the competition. However, smart companies gain market share by disrupting the influence of their competitors. They do this by introducing new ideas or reinventing the wheel. The larger market disruption you cause, the larger market share you win (don't forget the principle of survival of the fittest. If you are an entrepreneur, this is where this theory becomes reality).

Key learning objectives should include the reader's understanding of the following

- Which industry best fits your company

- Direct and indirect Competitors

- Porter's Five Forces Analysis

7.1 Which Industry Best Fits Your Company?

Knowing who your competitors are in the niche market, what they are selling and the methods they are using will help to develop a market strategy to grow your own business and make your brand stand out.

The ability to properly identify and monitor your competitors will help you with a wealth of knowledge about the market space. You can then use the knowledge gained to create marketing strategies that capitalize on your competitors' weaknesses and improve business performance. You can also assess the threats posed by both new entrants and existing competitors. This is to be truthful to yourself about how successful you can be in the niche.

It might be a new product or service that you need to sell or license before someone else gets their hands on it.

'The Art of War' is a systematic guide to strategy and tactics for rulers and commanders. The book discusses various tricks and the effect of terrain on the outcome of battles. It stresses the importance of accurate information about the enemy's forces, dispositions and deployments, and movements. This is summarized in the axiom "Know the enemy and know yourself, and you can fight a hundred battles with no danger of defeat." Sun Tzu (770–476 BC)

For your business to break even, it must be competitive with others in the same market. To do this you must know who to compete with and how to compete. Any smart business owner will monitor the competitive landscape of the market.

Potential Places to Find Competitors

Here are a few places where it is possible to easily identify potential competitors:

- Local corporate directory that is closer to your business

- Local chamber of commerce

- Commercial advertisements on Television, YouTube, Facebook etc

- Press release e.g Wall Street Journal, USA Today, The New York Times, etc

- Local and international exhibitions and trade fairs. Check out which of your competitors are also exhibiting.

- Academic journals

- Competitors' websites. This is because corporate websites often provide a wealth of information that companies traditionally do not disclose.

- Conduct questionnaires on existing customers. Tailor the questions according to the information you want to harvest.

- Search the Internet for similar products or services. The Internet can give you ample information on what companies around the world are doing in your niche.

- Flyers and marketing newsletter

The Internet and Competitors

Now that Information and Communication Technology (ICT) has been introduced into the business processes, all companies are in competition. Even a lonely restaurant in town will compete with other businesses such as cinemas, bars, and others where the customers spend their money. With the increased use of the Internet, it is no longer news that you may find yourself competing with companies from other countries. The likes of Aliexpress, eBay, and Amazon easily come to mind. The competitors may be a new company somewhere around the globe offering a replacement or similar product that will make yours obsolete. The earlier one realizes that "business war" exists, the better you prepare to stand your ground, because the competition is not just another business that can take cash from you but that which can also make your services/products irrelevant with time.

Get closer to your competitors

Here are a few tips to get closer to your competitors:

1. Don't just look for those that already exist; you also need to consistently lookout for potential new entrants in the market.

2. Make it a habit to occasionally call and ask for a copy of your competitors' brochures, request a price list or quantity discounts for standard items. This will give you an idea of how the competitors are winning their customers.

3. If possible, schedule a visit to the companies and have face-to-face contacts to help determine how they relate with people and the first impression they make on customers.

4. You may also encounter competitors at social or corporate events; talk to them and be friendly as much as possible - they are competitors, not enemies.

5. Develop the habit of listening to your customers, and don't just ask them how well you're satisfying their demands but ask which other companies they're patronizing.

6. Take the advantage of meeting with your suppliers and asking what their other customers are doing. You might not have all the information you want to know, but it's a useful start.

7. Ensure you jot down notes during all these discussions. You might discover a goldmine of information to help your business.

Competitors are not enemies

Remember, competitors are not your enemies but opponents that make the game lively. They can be equated to opponents in a sporting competition or political parties in an election; without them, the game is almost useless. A good example is the 2022 Commonwealth Games in Birmingham, UK. The joy of the game is in competing with others. Even though they started at the same time under the same condition, a particular candidate will always emerge to be leading the competition while others contend along.

Answer these questions honestly

To ensure your business competes competitively, you must honestly consider and provide appropriate answers to the following questions:

1. What are the irresistible offers your competitors are offering their customers?

2. How much are they charging for providing these offers? Can you provide the same or better product/service at a reduced price and still make a profit?

3. Who exactly are their customers? For example students, artists, civil servants, youths, adults, nursing mothers,

sportsmen, etc.

4. How are they marketing their product or service? Is it via newsprint, radio, TV, Facebook, YouTube, WhatsApp, Instagram, LinkedIn, etc?

5. Are they passionate about new products appearing in the market? You will easily know this via their advertisement. A serious competitor would want to advertise new products as soon as they are available.

6. How do they distribute or deliver their product/service? For example, do they add home delivery in distributing to their customers?

7. How many staff are on their payroll?

8. What caliber of staff do they attract into their workforce?

9. What sort of person owns the business? Is it sole proprietorship or partnership, billionaire or multinational etc? This will help to imagine their financial strength.

10. Their annual report - if they're a public company, read a copy of their annual report.

11. Do they have an online presence? For example, their website or email sent to their customers may reveal other hidden information. You can even ask for a trial of their service online and subscribe to their mailing list. Is there anything you could improve on for your own website after checking theirs?

12. What do customers see as your competitors' strengths and weaknesses?

The last and one question you have to provide a sincere answer to is:

13. Will you be passionate and consistent enough to continue to provide solutions to people's problems with little or no financial benefits? As we pointed out in Chapter 1, "Even though most entrepreneurs hope to make money from their businesses, they didn't set out to create cash-making machines from the onset..." This question is the key factor because even if you can provide answers to all the other 12 questions, without passion and consistency in what you are doing, sooner or later the heat wave of being an entrepreneur will sweep you out into history.

7.2 Paying Serious Attention to Your Direct and Indirect Competitors

You should watch out for the following types of competitors:

1. **A direct competitor** — A direct competitor is the first name that comes to mind when thinking of a competitor. These are businesses that provide the same products and services and target the same audience on a daily basis in your area or neighborhood. For example, if you are into hotel services, your direct competitors are all other hotels in the area. Other examples, at a global scale, are search engine websites such as Yahoo!, Bing, Ask, and Google. When customers log in to search for information, each of these search engines offer similar solutions.

2. **Indirect competitors** — Indirect competitors are difficult to easily identify. They serve the same customer needs as your business, but in a different way. Their target customers may overlap with your target audience, with a little difference.

To be considered an indirect competitor, a company must offer different products or services to meet the needs of the same target market. For example, two fast-food restaurants located in the same neighborhood (a pizzeria and a sandwich shop) are indirect competitors. Both offer food for low-income customers with convenience, but with different solutions. Although a customer who is seeking one will not be satisfied with the other.

Other competitors

Aside from the direct and indirect competitors discussed above, other competitors to watch out for are:

3. **Substitute competitors** — Substitute competitors do not sell comparable products, but compete for consumer spending without offering the same service. For example, fast food restaurants, bars, cafes, and supermarkets will all compete for customers during lunchtime within the same locality.

4. **New entrant** — New entrant is a new competitor entering the market and offering the same product or service. As entry is restricted, new entrants may find it easy or difficult to break into existing businesses. The easier it is for new competitors to have access to the market, the greater the risk for established businesses to lose market share. Examples are startup businesses around the country.

7.3 Undertaking Porter's Five Forces Analysis

Porter's Five Forces model is one of the ways to identify the competition and understand how you are faring in the market.

Originally developed in 1979 by Michael E. Porter of Harvard Business School, the Five Forces model examines five specific factors that determine whether a company is profitable compared to other companies in the same industry. Using Porter's Five Forces will help you understand where your company or business fits within the business environment.

It is critical to know who your competitors are and how their products, services, and marketing strategies affect yours. Even if your business is a multinational company or a startup, competition has a direct impact on your success as an entrepreneur. Porter hypothesized that it is important to understand both the current competitive environment and the overall business model in order to develop sound and creative decisions and competitive strategies for the future.

The five forces that shape industry competition are:

1. **Competitive Rivalry**

   This force looks at how competitive the market is. It considers how many competitors are in the market and what each can do. The competition is intense when only a few companies are rendering a service or product. The market will expand with consumers switching among competing products at lower prices. Often, competition can lead to fierce advertising and sales wars that can hurt a company's performance

   The main driver here is the number and capacity of competitors in the market. Too many competitors offering identical products and services reduce market attractiveness.

2. **Suppliers Bargaining Power**

   This force analyzes how much power a company's supplier has and how much control they have over their ability to increase prices at will, which in turn reduces the company's profits. It also assesses the number of suppliers of raw materials and other available resources. The smaller the supplier, the more power they exert when supplying raw materials to the company. Firms are in a better position if there are more suppliers, which in turn reduces the cost of production.

3. **Customer's Bargaining Power**

   This force examines how easy it is for buyers to drive prices down. The consumers influence the market when they are fewer as against the number of producers. This gives the consumers the power to change among the many competitors, especially when the buying power of the customer is low and the seller's product is very different from that of its competitors. When a business has only a few powerful buyers, they are often able to dictate the condition of the market.

4. **Threat of Substitution**

   This force examines how easy it is for consumers to switch from a business's product or service to that of a competitor. If close substitutes exist in the market, customers are more likely to switch to alternatives as prices increase. This reduces both supplier power and market attractiveness.

5. **Threat of New Entrants**

   This force takes into account how easy or difficult it is for competitors to enter the market. The easier it is for new competitors to enter, the greater the risk of an established company losing market share.

Quiz

1. **New entrant entrepreneurs are:**

   a. Those who are just entering a business niche afresh

   b. Those that have spent years at the entrance of a business

   c. Those who are in the business for many years

2. **A successful entrepreneur needs to find ways:**

   a. To cheat others in the market

   b. To stay ahead of the competition

   c. To play with the competitors

3. **Which of these is true about substitute competitors?**

   a. Customers are more likely not to buy from the new entrants

   b. Customers are more likely to switch to alternatives as prices increase.

   c. The substitute competitor will always win the market.

4. **The Five Forces model examines five specific factors that determine whether a _____**

   a. market is profitable enough to go global

   b. company is making profits every day or not

   c. company is profitable compared to other companies in the same industry

5. _____ is the first name that comes to mind when thinking of a competitor.

   a. New Entrant competitor

   b. Indirect competitor

   c. Direct competitor

6. Competitors are not one of the following:

   a. Enemies

   b. Friends

   c. Relatives

7. This is one of the ways to identify your competitors

   a. How many houses have they bought altogether

   b. How many children do they have

   c. How do they distribute or deliver their product/service

8. Ensure you _____ during your discussions while finding out more about your competitors

   a. jot notes

   b. smile always

   c. display your products

9. You may encounter business competitors at any of these places except _____

    a. exhibitions

    b. corporate events

    c. your home

10. Because of the introduction of _____ all companies are in competition.

    a. ICT

    b. TIC

    c. TTC

Answers	1 – a	2 – b	3 – b	4 – c	5 – c
	6 – a	7 – c	8 – a	9 – c	10 – a

Chapter Summary

◆ It is imperative that you identify both your direct and indirect competitors, most especially those operating in the same niche or industry as yours.

◆ It is a wrong assumption to consider your competitor as an enemy—they are, in fact, not your enemies. It is common for competitors to work together when designing an innovative product or service. Think of Apple, Inc. working with Microsoft.

◆ Porter's Five Forces - Competitive Rivalry, Suppliers Bargaining Power, Customer's Bargaining Power, Threat of Substitution, Threat of New Entrants This analysis is a very useful tool in identifying your competitors in the market and understanding your strength and capacity to compete with them

◆ It is important that you research your competitors and study how they carry out their operational activities and distribution.

◆ Indirect competitors are difficult to identify, but you should make an effort to know who they are.

References

- Sun Tzu (770–476 B retrieved from www.britannica.com

- Clyde Bank Media (2022, August 20). What is an indirect competitor? Retrieved from www.clydebankmedia.com

This page is intentionally left blank

Chapter **8**

Your Business Model

A company's business model is its operational "system or design" through which it can successfully identify its revenue sources, manage its product production and distribution, undertake customer management, and accountably manage its financial procedures.

A business without a clearly defined business model is comparable to a blindfolded person wandering aimlessly in the forest. It would be practically difficult for a business to pragmatically run its day-to-day operations, measure its progress, and plan for innovation without a well-structured business model.

Key learning objectives should include the reader's understanding of the following

- What is a business model and how can you develop it
- Strategic business operations
- Top-notch marketing activities
- Financial accountability and other related issues

8.1 What Is a Business Model and How Can You Develop It?

Knowing and understanding the exact problem you are solving for your customers is the biggest challenge you'll encounter in your market niche as a startup entrepreneur. However, this is just the starting point because you need to figure out how you're going to make money. What is the essence of a business without profit? To achieve business success, this is where you need to develop a Business Model.

A business model is an outline of how a company will create value for products or services delivered. It provides answers to essential questions about the problem you are going to solve, how you will solve it, and the growth opportunities within a given market. The business model is important whether you are starting a new venture, expanding into a new market, or changing your market strategy. It allows entrepreneurs to experiment, test, and model different ways of organizing costs and generating streams of income.

For new entrants, exploring existing business models can help determine if a business idea is viable, attract investors, and guides overall management strategies. And for established companies, it serves as the basis for developing financial projections, setting milestones and baselines for reviewing business plans.

A business model usually describes an entire business using visual images on one page, whereas a business plan describes a business in a longer document, which typically includes:

- description of the customer,

- details of how the customer will use the product,

- how the product will be sold,

- how the business will be promoted.

- key operational tasks e.g staffing, etc

- details on how the business operates.

Discussion Question:
Can a company that lacks a well-designed Business Model outlast its competitors?

The Business Model Canvas (BMC) Building Blocks

Dr. Yves Pigneur invented the Business Model Canvas (BM with Osterwalder and authored an international bestseller in 2010 called "Business Model Generation," selling over 10 million copies.

Pigneur and Osterwalder identified nine building blocks that are critical dimensions for every business venture in the 21st century, which is a way of thinking through multiple elements for either new or existing ventures:

However, Paul Myers, MBA renumbered these building blocks, as shown below, for better implementation:

No 1. — Customers Segment

Which segment of customers are you targeting so as to create some value for them?

Who are your most ideal customers?

No 2. — Value Proposition

What are the core values associated with your business?

What kind of value are you delivering to the consumer?

What are you doing to meet or exceed your customers' expectations?

No 3. — Distribution Channel

What distribution channels do you employ in reaching out to your customers?

What are your customers' most preferable channels?

What distribution channels are the most effective for you?

What are their costs?

How can you integrate them into your customers' daily routines?

No 4. — Customer Relationships

What are your customer's expectations as far as the relationship is concerned?

How will you be able to incorporate this into your business cost and format?

No 5. — Revenue Stream

What core values are your customers excited about and ready to pay for?

What payment methods will you adopt?

What are your customers' payment preferences?

How much do you make from each revenue stream per a certain period?

No 6. — Key Resources

What are the required resources for delivering your value proposition?

What are the most essential resources needed for effective customer relationships, distribution channels, revenue streams, and so on?

No 7. — Key Activities

What key activities do you engage in to deliver your value proposition?

What activities are necessary for achieving effective customer relationships, distribution channels, revenue streams, and so on?

No 8. — Key Partners

Who are your business's major partners or suppliers?

What are the main factors responsible for maintaining this relationship/partnership?

No 9. — Cost Structure

What are the main costs for running your business?

Which major resources and activities are costing your business a lot of money?

Remember that BMC is a dynamic process that can evolve to a desirable state over time.

Steps to Create a Business Model

1. Collect and evaluate information about your business to create a visual description of how the business looks. Ensure to keep the business model as simple as possible. You can

start by looking at the problem you're going to solve and limit your choice to three key problems your product and service will solve.

2. Be specific about your business goals and your plan to attract customers who can pay a profitable price for your products or services. Successful business models target the right demographics with low marketing expenses.

3. Identify the central aspect of what exactly your company is trying to offer. An effective business model relies on being clear about the key features and benefits associated with a product or service. Show how your business wants to increase or maintain competitiveness through better distribution, better customer relationships, new customer solutions, lower prices, faster delivery, and so on.

4. Explain how you plan to make your business more efficient and produce better products than your competitors. For example, identify an opportunity to use better technology or process and if it is also possible to produce a better product outside your country.

5. In your business model, identify key partners such as suppliers, strategic alliances, or advertising agencies you can leverage on their strengths to satisfy your customers. No business can stay alone like an island.

6. How will your customers find you? What should they do once they are aware of your product or service? Developing a demand generation methodology creates a customer journey plan while documenting key motivations for their action.

8.2 Strategic Business Operations

Business operational strategies are used by organizations across all sectors to set short and long-term objectives and develop plans to accomplish them. To make sure that every area of an organization functions harmoniously, business strategy and operations may need to harmonize. Your business will accomplish its objectives and enhance decision-making by learning how to create an effective operational strategy.

What Is an Operational Business Strategy?

An operational business strategy is a decision-making process that shapes an organization's long-term plans to achieve the goals in its mission statement. It includes specific actions that management wishes to take in order to accomplish a particular aspect of a company's operations. Operational strategies connect the company's programs, policies, rules, and staff in a way that allows each branch to assist others in achieving a common goal. An effective business strategy takes into account a company's long-term goals and creates steps that consistently link business plans to resources, capacity, time, location, and competition. Successful implementation of the operational strategy strengthens the company's overall strategy and gives it a market advantage over its competitors. It can also improve the efficiency and infrastructure of the organization to better serve customers and maintain or increase competitive advantage over other companies in the market.

Types of Business Operational Strategies

Here are some common operational strategies that organizations can use to improve efficiency, function, and sustain competitive advantage.

- **Corporate strategy:** This comprises all the company and department-wide policies and guidelines required for smoothly running a company as a system. This strategy is used in guiding the day-to-day operations of the company since it unites the different divisions in the company around a common vision and mission.

- **Customer-centric operational strategy:** A company utilizes customer-centric strategy to obtain vital data about its customers, which may include their buying patterns or behaviors, trends, and preferences according to their demographics. The company can use the data to better serve its customers.

- **Basic competence strategy:** Companies utilize their basic competency strategy to highlight their main strengths, capabilities, and resources. These may include a company's proprietary technology, experienced employees, market share, distribution networks, and financial standing. Knowing its basic competencies can encourage a company to expand its operations, increase its customer base, meet its customers' expectations, and maintain a leading position in the market. or industry.

- **Competitive priorities strategies:** The best approach for companies to distinguish their brands, employees, products, and services from the other companies is to present their competitive advantages. . This may be seen in their organizational culture, production procedures, marketing approaches, and customer relationship. Using its competitive advantages, a company can make high-quality products for its customers and maintain a lead over its competitors.

- **A product or service development strategy:** With this strategy, a company can embrace greater innovation and improved production processes to make products/ services that will meet its customers' needs. This involves making effective use of resources, people, and geographical relevance.

- **Cost-driven strategies:** Companies can compete favorably with their competitors on price by adopting cost-driven strategies. This entails manufacturing products cost-effectively to be able to release products that can compete with others on pricing.

- **Outsourcing strategy:** To cut costs, a company may implement an outsourcing strategy whereby some aspects of their manufacturing are passed on to third parties that would do the jobs for them at a lower cost. This can help such a company to offer products/services that have a competitive pricing advantage in the market.

- **Flexibility strategy:** This strategy makes it possible for companies to compete with others by embracing some flexibility in their production and product development. This entails that a company can quickly make products that its customers need, even though such manufacturing activity was not previously planned. This is in contrast to the rigid production arrangement many companies have.

8.3 Top-Notch Marketing Activities

Marketing activities are strategies that help a company develop and promote its products or services to its customers. Companies use marketing activities to identify their target audience and develop or improve what they offer to meet their needs. With these strategies, companies achieve revenue targets, improve brand awareness and increase their customer base.

Benefits of Marketing Activities

The benefit of marketing activities includes:

- **Understanding a company's market:** It helps to understand the company's market by identifying the customers who are most likely to use its products or services. Information provided will help them to effectively market a company's product or service to its consumers.

- **Attracting customers:** Marketing is also used to direct specific messages to a company's target audience, attract new customers, and sustain good relationships with loyal customers.

- **Promote company's offerings:** Marketing can help to promote what a company offers through various channels while providing useful information about the value of the company's products or services.

- **Improve company's brand:** Marketing can help to improve the company's brand by distinguishing its products or services from its competitors, which in turn helps customers to remember a company in the future when purchasing similar products or services.

- **Grow business:** An effective marketing activity will help in generating new leads and boost sales, and subsequently help the company to successfully grow its business within a niche market.

7 Top-Notch Marketing Activities

Below are seven examples of marketing activities to help a company develop and promote its brand and stand out among its competitors:

- **Market research**
  Market research is very important to businesses because it is one of the commonest procedures for collecting important data about customers and learning about their behaviors and preferences. After the initial market research, a company can customize its products/services to exactly meet the needs of its customers. Essentially, market research can be conducted via surveys, questionnaires, interactions on social media, phone calls. etc.

- **Lead generation**
  Lead generation is all about encouraging prospective customers/clients to buy a product/service. It is important that their interests are stoked by offering attractive offers that could be displayed in advertisements or promotions. Once a handful of people start showing interest in the offers, they could be handed over to the marketing team who will handle the sales interaction with them. This is a major method for acquiring new customers for businesses.

- **Cold calling**

  Marketers can decide to call people's homes or offices at random to discuss their companies' products/services with them. This is referred to as cold calling. This has been one of the traditional approaches to marketing, but it could still yield some measurable results nowadays, and some of the prospective cold-called customers may eventually become loyal customers.

- **Advertising**

  Advertising helps businesses promote their products/ services to potential customers. In addition to the traditional advertising on TV, radio, and in newspapers, we now have digital marketing opportunities such as running Google ads, Facebook ads, etc. All these efforts are deployed into winning the hearts of prospective customers and serving them with exactly what they require.

- **Content marketing**

  Using blogs, newsletters, and website content, companies can market their brands to potential customers. When a person reads some information in a company's blog, he/ she may want to inquire about the products/services being described in the blog. It is one of the cheapest forms of marketing that many companies are using.

- **Search engine marketing**

  Using customer-centric keywords, a company can decide to target new customers based on what other people are searching for online. Search engines such as Google, Yahoo, and MSN are configured in a way that they could lead potential buyers to companies' websites that sell exactly the products/services that they need. This kind of marketing is also affordable to many businesses.

- **Sales promotions**
  Companies run sales promotions, competitions, giveaways, and offer freebies to attract new customers. This has been a long-running practice among many businesses.

8.4 Financial Accountability and Other Related Issues

Building on your financial literacy abilities is crucial when beginning or expanding your business to make sure you have a firm grasp of your financial records. With the correct talents, entrepreneurship can be a financially successful endeavor as well as an enjoyable one. Smart business owners will honestly take all reasonable steps to secure the success of their enterprise.

Entrepreneurs must be aware and put a demarcation between their personal and business finances. Doing so will help them monitor the progress of their businesses. This is because many entrepreneurs, particularly new business owners, rely on personal funding to support their enterprises.

Business owners can build a secure financial future by being familiar with the fundamental abilities needed to manage a small business, such as performing simple accounting activities, asking for a loan, or producing financial statements. Being organized is a key element of successful money management, along with financial education.

Tips for Managing Small Business Finances

- **Pay yourself**

  Small business owners are mostly encouraged to pay themselves first. This action can motivate entrepreneurs to work harder on their businesses if they are getting rewarded for the efforts they are putting into their businesses. More so, their financial and personal needs could be met and they wouldn't be distracted looking for money elsewhere, such as working for another business part-time.

- **Invest in growth**

  For any business to grow, there must be an ample investment in innovation and expansion. This may involve spending more money on product/service development and customization operations to meet modern demands.

- **Don't be afraid of loans**

  Taking loans from banks and other financial institutions should be seen in a positive light. It is a fact that businesses need money to survive; so, if you have access to some financial support in the form of loans, it is advisable that you accountably use them.

- **Keep good business credit**

  The best way a company can maintain a good business credit profile is to constantly pay off its existing debts. As a result of this, it may be possible for such a company to be offered new financial assistance in the course of its operations.

- **Have a good billing strategy**

  The primary purpose of having a good billing strategy is that businesses can know how much money is coming in and going out. It can also determine how much money it is owed by customers purchasing its products/services on credit. Every company aspires to achieve high liquidity status, and this can mainly be measured through an effective billing system.

- **Spread out tax payments**
  Paying all your business's taxes one time may put some pressure on your finances. You can decide to pay your taxes monthly, quarterly, or twice a year. All you need to do is to make arrangements about this with your country's or city's tax agencies.

- **Monitor your expenditures and Return-on-Investment (ROI).**
  A business needs to monitor its concurrent expenditures and the possible return on investment (ROI). By doing this, it can detect how its investments are performing. More so, it could know which areas of its business activities are doing well and need additional funding to make it grow.

- **Plan ahead.**
  Businesses need to plan ahead all their operational activities as well as the required finances to make them work. By taking this step, they could avoid running into an unforeseen financial problem while managing their company's activities.

Types of Business Finances

It's crucial to keep in mind that your business finances involve more than just your income; they also involve your spending habits and the sources of your funding. Debt funding and equity funding are the two primary funding types when it comes to where you obtain your funding:

- **Debt funding**

  Debt financing is one of the commonly used methods of financing businesses nowadays. A company may decide to sell its debts to a financial institution like a bank and then use the money to fund some of its operations. When repaid on time, such a business can have access to more funds from different financial institutions.

- **Equity funding**

  On the other hand, equity funding involves asking other people to invest in your business with a promise that they will own part of the business. A company can invite investors, venture capitalists, and crowdfunding equity holders to join them in financing its business activities. Those categories of investors will have some percentage ownership in the company after putting their hard-earned money into its operations.

Quiz

1. **It is a good practice to always take loans you**

   a. can pay back easily within a short time frame

   b. cannot pay back easily to run your business.

   c. can pay back easily to run your competitors down

2. **BMC is a _____ that can evolve to a desirable taste over time.**

   a. unpredictable business

   b. profitable venture

   c. dynamic process

3. **_____ are strategies that help a company develop and promote its products or services to its customers.**

   a. Business expenditure

   b. Marketing activities

   c. None of the above

4. **An effective marketing activity will help in _____**

   a. generating new leads and boosting sales

   b. making more noise about the business

   c. retaining talented employees

5. **One of the following is not a benefit of marketing activities**

    a. Improve the company's brand

    b. Understand the company's market

    c. Debt funding

6. **An _____ is a decision-making process that shapes an organization's long-term plans to achieve the goals in its mission statement.**

    a. operational business strategy

    b. equity funding

    c. marketing strategy

7. **Examples of traditional types of advertisement are:**

    a. Periodicals, newspapers, TV and radio commercials

    b. Business news and web searching

    c. Social media and online radio

8. **_____ is when an industry relies on the expertise and supply chain resources of others to produce their products and services and deliver them to their customers.**

    a. Foreign marketing

    b. Outsourcing Strategy

    c. Buying power

9. Cold calling can assist marketers in reaching out to ____ who may not have previously been aware of a company's goods or services.

    a. potential clients

    b. unserious clients

    c. uneducated clients

10. Operational strategies connect the company's programs, _____ in a way that allows each branch to assist others in achieving a common goal.

    a. policies, rules, and staff

    b. location, government, and state

    c. competitors, time, and fund

Answers	1 – a	2 – c	3 – b	4 – a	5 – c
	6 – a	7 – a	8 – b	9 – a	10 – a

Chapter Summary

◆ A business model is an outline of how a company will create value for products or services delivered. It provides essential questions about the problem you are going to solve, how you will solve it, and the growth opportunity within a given market.

◆ Pigneur and Osterwalder identified nine building blocks that are critical dimensions for every business venture in the 21st century.

◆ An operational business strategy is a decision-making process that shapes an organization's long-term plans to achieve the goals in its mission statement.

◆ Types of business operational strategies are corporate strategy, customer-centric operational strategy, basic competence strategy, competitive priorities strategy, product or service development strategy, cost-driven strategy, outsourcing strategy, and flexibility strategy.

◆ Top-notch marketing activities are strategies that help a company develop and promote its products or services to its customers.

◆ Entrepreneurs must be aware and put a demarcation between their personal and business finances. Doing so will help them to monitor the progress of their businesses

◆ Tips for managing your business finances include paying yourself, investing in growth, not being afraid of loans, keeping good business credit, having a goodbilling strategy, spreading out tax payments, planning ahead, and monitoring your expenditures and Return-on-Investment (ROI).

References

- I. AG, S., (2020): "Corporate Innovation Strategy, Tools & Training". Available at: www.strategyzer.com

- II. Indeed Editorial Team (2022): "Business Strategy and Operations: Definition, Types and Tips" . Indeed. Available at: www.indeed.com

- Matt D'Angelo (2022): "10 Tips for Managing Small Business Finances" Business News Daily. Available at: www. businessnewsdaily.com

- Melissa Houston (2021): "How Entrepreneurs Can Manage Their Business Finances With Success" Entrepreneur. Available at: www. entrepreneur.com

- Paul Myers MBA (2022): "How to Develop a Business Model for Your Startup". Available at: www.medium.com

Chapter **9**

Growing Your Company With Innovations

A company that fails to innovate is surely preparing itself for a sudden collapse. Many businesses that were reputable decades ago have lost their past glories. For example, Nokia, Kodak, Xerox, and Blackberry Motion are no longer around because they refused to embrace innovations when other players in their industries were utilizing new inventions to drive sales and maintain customer satisfaction.

Key learning objectives should include the reader's understanding of the following

- The merits of corporate/company culture

- Team building

- How innovations make businesses thrive

- Change planning and management

9.1 The Merits of Corporate/Company Culture

What is Corporate/Company Culture

The term "corporate culture" describes the attitudes, standards, and general conduct of employees as well as how they relate to one another. It also covers how management and staff deal with other parties like customers or independent vendors. Corporate culture is an unclear impression about the company that is assumed rather than stated clearly. It evolves naturally over time, and everyone involved learns from and adjusts to it.

This may include a way of evaluating how employees interact with one another, how they celebrate victories, and how management encourages improvement. When a company's culture is well-defined, over time, it will attract like-minded experts who will flourish in the type of environment that has been created.

Merits of Corporate/Company Culture

- **Staff retention**
  Morale is higher in organizations that cherish their workers and place a high priority on creating a positive corporate culture. Positive attitudes among employees about their workplace are more likely to keep them with the company and invariably reduce the need for hiring and training new staff. This in turn lowers the cost of human resources.

- **Reputation**

  Clients, employees, and the general public have a favorable perception of companies with healthy corporate cultures. It also draws talented, like-minded professionals. Companies with a solid reputation can charge more for their goods and services, raising the overall worth of the business. Also, customers may choose to patronize a more reputable company while paying more.

- **Employee unity**

  When forming their ideas on a workplace's corporate culture, employees naturally take signals from management while new hires observe how current employees behave. Once everyone adopts a habit, a culture develops and links between workers and management are strengthened. Employees who are unified experience a sense of belonging to a team. A unified corporate culture logically urges employees to place greater emphasis on the company's overall success than just their own successes.

- **Better decision-making**

  Employees are encouraged to make wiser decisions by an established corporate culture that is based on common goals, visions, and values. In the end, they have a distinct impression of the company and what it stands for, which can act as a guide in their decision-making.

- **Enhances company brand**

  Sharing your company's cultural values on social media and the website will help you build your brand. Even though the company's culture ought to be clear to all employees, highlighting it even further wouldn't hurt, especially if it were to show in the organization's performance. What damage would it do to try to manage this a little bit more carefully given that how people perceive your company has the power to make or break it?

9.2 Team Building

Team building is the act of turning a group of individual contributors into a cohesive team —a group of people structured to work together to realize their purpose and goals, from a collection of individuals who each contribute to the team is known as team building.

Team building strengthens the connections between group members. The individual members appreciate one another's differences as well as their own, and they all have similar expectations and aspirations.

Advantages of Team-Building

The advantages of team building include improved collaboration, planning abilities, employee engagement and communication, problem-solving, and conflict resolution. Getting results is one of the most compelling justifications for team building.

Some advantages of team-building include:

- Building trust and inclusivity among the team

- Motivating team members

- Getting to know colleagues better

- Stimulating creativity and empowering new ideas

- Learning new skills and processes

- Becoming better problem-solvers

- Increasing team unity

- Decreasing stress and have fun together

- Improved collaboration

- Improved communication problem-solving

- Conflict resolution

9.3 How Innovations Make Businesses Thrive

Markets at all levels—local, regional, national, and international—are becoming more competitive. Wider access to new technology and the expanded commerce and knowledge-sharing opportunities provided by the Internet have intensified competition.

The process of introducing new procedures, services, or goods into organizations is known as business innovation.

The main objective of this kind of innovation is to encourage constructive internal changes. To stay competitive in the niche market, a company must successfully utilize new ideas (innovation) in order to advance its operations by introducing fresh products and services to the market, boosting productivity, and most significantly, raising profits. Innovation need not involve a discovery that alters the course of history. It could mean making small, gradual improvements in any area of your business. It could be a strategy for a better good or service, an updated way of managing your business, or even a new business model. It doesn't necessarily have to be novel—it may have already been used at another company—and it can apply to any aspect of your organization.

Types of Innovations

1. **Incremental innovation**

   These are minor adjustments that make your present business model more effective. You may, for instance, modify your procedures, expand your digital offerings, reduce expenses, or improve your goods and services in the near future.

2. **Expansive innovation**

   This transformation is the outcome of considering fresh concepts. Its goal is to sustain and expand the business in the long term. In this case, a company explores new depths and territories that its competitors avoid.

   Science and technology are typically linked to expansive innovation. The Internet of Things (IoTs) or artificial intelligence (AI) will be used in many of the breakthroughs we're already witnessing. In addition to testing and prototyping, expansive innovation also entails changing the business model. Implementing a change of business model may take up to 12 to 24 months before completion.

3. **Disruptive innovation**

   A disruptive innovation is one that introduces a brand new business model with a distinctive value proposition.

   It refers to creating or redesigning a product or service. There is a lot of uncertainty even though the benefits could be huge. When effective, this kind of invention takes three to five years to develop.

Stages of Innovation

There are three (3) stages involved in innovation:

1. **Design stage**

   This is the moment to brainstorm new business models or ways to deal with innovative products or services. The next step is to create a prototype that will eventually become your minimum viable product, meaning it will have sufficient functionality to draw early customers or investors.

2. **Testing stage**

   Here is where you rapidly test the modified versions of your concept. You will discover what works and what doesn't. The idea can be tested with prospective users and consumers. This will present you with the chance to modify your approach before you proceed too far and it becomes more difficult to make modifications. Actually, this stage is a stage of risk management.

3. **Scaling stage**

   This is when you are prepared to scale up after the design and testing has demonstrated how your innovation can address a genuine issue. In practice, this entails creating a thorough business plan based on data, expanding the market for your product or service, and implementing a targeted promotional campaign.

9.4 Change Planning and Management

A change management plan is a roadmap outlining specific actions a business will take to implement and carry out the change management process.

Organizations create change management plans to accept and deal with changes in their workflow. It explains how to use the tools and procedures needed to manage people in order to change the environment.

This plan not only lays out the strategy for implementing the change, but also considers the impact it will have on the project or organization, the processes, and your interactions with clients or team members. It assists you in maintaining control over the finances, timeline, scope, resources, and communication system.

Even though business change is common, not all change initiatives will be successful. This frequently occurs because the managers who work directly with customers are not the main emphasis or because those managers are unsure of the precise steps they must take to succeed. Change management is advantageous for companies that want to implement change successfully.

The larger effects of change are also a focus of change management, along with how people and teams adapt to the new environment. Change management can deal with minor process adjustments as well as significant shifts in strategy or policy. The overall objective is to have a clear strategy that everyone should understand, hence facilitating adjustments more easily. Making sure everyone is on the same page and that the changes are beneficial and pleasant entails checking in with the staff. When an organization uses change management, better results will probably follow.

Best Practices for Change Management

There are several procedures you can put in place to make sure the changes your firm will experience are beneficial and significant. Among these best practices are:

- Encourage open dialogue so that workers feel free to express their emotions.

- Be open and honest about forthcoming modifications or shifts.

- Create a change-friendly workplace culture.

- Develop reporting schedules so that stakeholders can track the progress of changes.

- If adjustments need to be made, consider hiring a new project manager or consultant.

- Establishing effective reporting tools and systems early will help your firm choose the best strategy to track change.

Quiz

1. _____ is the act of turning a group of individual contributors into a cohesive team.

    a. Business partner

    b. Football team

    c. Team building

2. Getting _____ is one of the most compelling justifications for team building.

    a. employees Benefits

    b. results

    c. information

3. One of the advantages of team building includes _____

    a. conflict resolution

    b. conflict escalation

    c. conflict renegotiation

4. Innovation could mean _____ in any area of your business.

    a. giant discovery

    b. making small, gradual improvements

    c. securing equity debt

5. A unified _____ logically urges employees to place greater emphasis on the company's overall success than just their own successes.

   a. corporate culture

   b. attitude

   c. customer

6. _____ is not one of the advantages of team building

   a. Improved collaboration

   b. Planning abilities

   c. Taxation

7. Business Innovation need not involve a _____ that alters the course of history.

   a. product

   b. service

   c. discovery

8. Making minor adjustments that make your present business model more effective is known as_____

   a. incremental innovation

   b. adjustment innovation

   c. purposeful innovation

9. A _____ is one that introduces a brand-new business model with a distinctive value proposition.

    a. disruptive innovation

    b. constant innovation

    c. linear innovation

10. _____ is frequently an unclear impression about the company that is assumed rather than stated clearly.

    a. Conflict resolution

    b. Corporate culture

    c. Loan repayment

Answers	1 – c	2 – b	3 – a	4 – b	5 – a
	6 – c	7 – c	8 – a	9 – a	10 – b

Chapter Summary

◆ The term "corporate culture" describes the attitudes, standards, and general conduct of employees as well as how they relate to one another. It also covers how management and staff deal with other parties like customers or independent vendors.

◆ Merits of Corporate/Company Culture: staff retention; reputation; employee unity; better decision-making and enhanced company brand.

◆ Team building strengthens the connections between group members. The individual members appreciate one another's differences as well as their own, and they all have similar expectations and aspirations.

◆ Innovation need not involve a discovery that alters the course of history. It could mean making small, gradual improvements in any area of your business. It could be a strategy for a better good or service, an updated way of managing your business, or even a new business model.

◆ Types of innovation are Incremental innovation, Expansive innovation, and Disruptive innovation.

References

- Indeed Editorial Team (2020): "Corporate Culture Examples and Benefits" Indeed. Available at: www.indeed.com

- Adam Gutman (2022) "What is innovation" BDC. available at: www.bdc.ca.com

- WGU (2020): "What is change management and how does it work?" WGU. Available at: www.wgu.edu.com

- Judy Lindenberger (2018): "8 Ways to Manage Change in Workplace Effectively". Available at: www.lindenbergergroup.com

Chapter **10**

Your Value Proposition

Every company or business must demonstrate certain values that its current and prospective customers can identify. Customers will remain loyal to your business if they are certainly deriving value from the solutions you are offering.

Even though a company or business produces value in the products/services it makes available to its customers, it is imperative that such a business should promote its value so that future customers could know about it and possibly embrace the company's products/services.

How can a business successfully undertake its value proposition? What does a business stand to gain from actively promoting its products' or services' value?

Key learning objectives should include the reader's understanding of the following

- The power of value proposition

- How your products/services can become household names

- Thinking like a consumer

10.1 The Power of Value Proposition

Essentially, a value proposition is a process of stating or promising the exact value a customer will gain by utilizing a company's product/service. In other words, it is releasing the benefits a customer will derive from using the product/service. Nike promotes its shoes as sleek, fast, and light. In the same way, Apple, Inc. promises a smartphone (iPhone) that seamlessly combines telephony with internet services. So, when customers are looking for a particular product/service, they will first read what the manufacturer says the product will do. If it meets their needs, they may go ahead to purchase the product or sign up for the service.

So, how powerful is the value proposition for businesses? Imagine you enter a drugstore looking for some supplements that can help you lose weight. If your eyes roam to the section named "Weight loss supplements", your feet will carry you as fast as possible in that direction. Standing in front of the section, you will still want to know more about the effectiveness of each weight loss supplement by reading their labels and other applicable information provided about them. If you then see a supplement that promises "quick weight loss with no side effects!" that may likely be your final choice. Why? It is because the supplement can help you lose weight while inflicting no adverse or harmful effects on your health.

That's how powerful the value proposition is! Apple, Inc. is not the only company producing smartwatches or smartphones in the world, yet due to the usefulness of its products' features, they are always sold out when launched or released into the market.

10.2 How Your Products/Services Can Become Household Names

If you are wondering how some products become household names while others, even better ones, don't, you will discover that what makes the difference is the way those unpopular products were positioned to customers.

As an entrepreneur, to make your products/services become household names, you need to carry out the following procedures:

i. **Identifying your actual customers and what they need:** From your initial market analysis, you would have properly identified the market segments that exactly need what your company is going to manufacture or produce. For example, if you have discovered that there are a lot of people who suffer from after-shower rashes after using soap and other body creams, you can develop a product that will help them get over that problem. It is those happy customers that will help you introduce your great product to other friends and families that may be suffering from the same problem. Hence, to become a household name, you should have clearly indicated the benefits every user stands to gain from your product on its label and product information. When marketing the product, it is this comparative quality that your marketing message will be harping on.

ii. **Clarity and conciseness matter:** You don't have a lot of space on your product information label to explain its benefits to prospective customers. So, you should provide concise and clear details that are enough to summarize what users can gain from using it. This is where your top-notch marketing team must apply their creativity. They must provide a catchy or attractive description that invokes curiosity in consumers to the extent that they will be interested in knowing more about the usefulness of your products. Examples of household products with catchy product slogans and taglines include Apple's "Think Different," L'oreal's ``Because you're worth it," McDonald's' "I'm loving it!" and Nike's "Just do it!" These product slogans attract consumers' attention immediately and cause them to investigate more about the products.

iii. **Physical appearance or designs:** Consumers sumers show tremendous interest in products not only because they offer great benefits, but also because they are attractive or presentable. Have you ever got to a store, got interested in buying something, maybe bread, and your eyes got attracted to the one with exquisite design and labeling? Well, most consumers act in the same or similar way. How you package your product is also another technique for putting it right in front of inquisitive consumers who may want to check it out. It is not uncommon to see people go into a store with the intention of buying a product only to change their minds when they discover another attractive and more popular one in the store. Do you know that beauty and luxury products/services are patronized based on their designs and attractiveness? The truth is that it doesn't matter how much you are spending on advertisements or how useful your product is; if your product packaging is shabby and unattractive, consumers will avoid it like a disease.

iv. **What's in a name?** Very few entrepreneurs understand that the names they give to their products/services matter a lot to consumers. Imagine entering a beauty store to buy a body cream, and you see two products on the shelf. One of the products is called "Elegance" and the other is named "Muffins". Your instinct will be to check out the "elegance" body cream before proceeding to have a look at the "muffins" body cream if at all you want to. Today, businesses thrive on the name they have built for themselves for decades. Car companies like Toyota, Ford, and BMW will forever remain engrained in people's memory; it doesn't matter how innovative and modern the newest car companies are.

v. **Be all ears to your customers:** Your product may not come out perfect in its first version or release, but it can gradually develop into becoming a great product when you take your customers' complaints into consideration. Once you give customers what they want, your product is likely going to be praised and promoted everywhere by happy users. No amount of advertisement spending can outperform word-of-mouth promotion. That is why successful companies establish seamless communication with their customers so that they can interact productively with them.

10.3 Thinking Like a Consumer

If you are a customer, what does a company need to do before you can fall in love with their products/services and become their unpaid promoter?

Before your product can become a household name, there must be a large number of loyal customers that are willing and ready to spread the word about how great and beneficial your product is to their friends and others.

So, what do customers really want from your business? According to Shannon Gronich, a customer deserves to be served the following:

a. **High quality:** The inherent quality of your product/service must be better than those of your competitors' products. It doesn't matter what you claim that your product can do for consumers, if it lacks the expected quality no one will purchase it. How will you feel buying a product that lacks the necessary active ingredients? You can package it well, and use flowing slogans to promote it, but the product will still flop because it doesn't contain what customers exactly need.

b. **Customization:** Nowadays, people spend their hard-earned money on products that align with their lifestyles and daily requirements. Years ago, you would use an antiseptic soap for bathing as well as shaving. Now, there are countless shaving soaps, and people with beards are more likely to go for that than trying antiseptic soaps.

c. **Trustworthy product:** Your customers are ready to be diehard customers for your product/service if they find it to be reliable and of great value. On most occasions, companies don't necessarily need to beg their customers to help promote their products/services. When customers realize they have discovered a very useful product, out of their own volition, they are willing to announce the product to the world.

d. **Convenience:** If your product makes life better for your customers, they are likely going to introduce it to their loved ones who might enjoy the same amount of convenience. When consumers notice that your products/services have removed their pain points or problems, they have no option but to tell someone else about them.

e. **Simplicity and affordability:** Your product must be simple for consumers to use. No one will be interested in recommending a very complex product to others. Moreso, your product/service must be affordable—this means that an expensive product if it is not a luxury product, may discourage people from purchasing it.

Quiz

1. **What does it mean for a product/service to become a household name?**

   a. Everyone knows it

   b. No one knows it

   c. I don't know

2. **Loyal customers will help you promote your great products/ services.**

   a. True

   b. False

   c. I don't know

3. **Word of mouth is the most effective and cheapest marketing for your product.**

   a. False

   b. True

   c. I don't know

4. **Why should entrepreneurs think like their customers?**

   a. So that they can spend money like their customers.

   b. To determine what motivates their customers to buy their products.

   c. To change themselves into their own customers.

5. **Why should a product be affordable to consumers?**

   a. So that the entrepreneur making it should lose money.

   b. The product should be considered a gift to consumers.

   c. The more people who buy it, the more people can spread the word about it.

6. **How important is a product's quality to consumers?**

   a. Not very important.

   b. It is very important.

   c. People don't care about a product's quality.

7. **Which of these processes may not help your product to become a household name?**

   a. Not identifying the right market segment to sell your product to.

   b. Making high-quality products available to your customers.

   c. Making it very simple for your customers to use your product.

8. **Why is it important for businesses to have a good customer relationship system?**

   a. They can be all ears to their customers.

   b. So that they can fight their customers.

   c. So that they can reject unused products customers returned to the company.

9. Customers are usually happy to purchase a product that brings them_____

    a. sadness

    b. convenience

    c. discomfort

10. If your product/service has great value, your customers will willingly introduce it to their friends and families.

    a. I don't think so

    b. True

    c. False

Answers	1 – a	2 – a	3 – b	4 – b	5 – c
	6 – b	7 – a	8 – a	9 – b	10 – b

Chapter Summary

◆ Your value proposition tells current and prospective customers what they can benefit from using your products/services.

◆ To know how consumers feel about a certain product/ service, it is advisable that entrepreneurs should put themselves in the position of consumers and think like them.

◆ Loyal customers will be attracted to your products/ services if they offer value, good quality, affordability, simplicity, convenience, and reliability.

◆ Knowing who your true customers are is the first step in making your product turn into a household name.

◆ It is also believed that your product's/service's name, worthiness, design, or packaging can influence the way customers patronize it.

References

- CFI (2022, February 27). Value proposition. Available at: www. corporatefinanceinstitute.com

- Gronich, S. (2021, September 23). What do customers want from your business? Available at: www.shannongronich.com

- Scudamore, B. (2015, December 15). 4 tips to create a household name, not just a brand. Available at: www.forbes.com

Chapter 11

How Sustainable Is Your Company?

Let's assume you have successfully set up a flourishing business/company, manufactured your great product, marketed them to prospective customers, and maintained good rapport with your customers to achieve constant patronage and generate recurrent revenues. Pat yourself on the back for a job well done as an entrepreneur.

However, entrepreneurship, as they say, isn't a sprint; it is indeed a marathon. Some companies have been in existence for fifty or hundred years or more. Are you sure your current business is sustainable as it is and can achieve longevity like other long-standing companies?

Key learning objectives should include the reader's understanding of the following

- Corporate sustainability
- Ethics, Standards, and Regulations (obey all the laws of the Land!)

• Business Bootstrapping

11.1 Understanding the Concept of Corporate Sustainability

The concept of corporate sustainability is all about incorporating long-term corporate values into your company's routine operations for the singular purpose of making it outlast its competitors. There are three intrinsic pillars of all corporate sustainability— environmental, social, and governance (ESG).

i. **Environmental aspect:** This entails that your company must identify and strictly comply with all environmental regulations or laws in your jurisdiction of operations. For instance, governments are encouraging businesses to pay serious attention to their activities and desist from doing anything that could increase carbon emissions and exacerbate the existing global warming problem. More so, your company should engage in activities that could lead to an acute reduction in pollution, and unsustainable use of water and other marine resources, while promoting the protection of biodiversity and ecosystems. In other words, entrepreneurs are advised to find raw materials from renewable and/recyclable sources. This serves to help a business obtain raw materials from sources that naturally regenerate without any hassles.

ii. **Social aspect:** The social aspect of corporate sustainability focuses on the relationship of your company with its employees, partners, vendors, customers, suppliers, and in general the communities where your business(s) are located. If your company is set to stand the test of time, it must pay attention and properly manage labor relations, human rights issues, diversity and inclusion requirements, and safety and health issues pertaining to its employees and other people that are connected with the company. A company doesn't stand on its own: it is connected to several people, both internal and external influencers. Hence, all these people must be treated fairly as required by laws.

iii. **Governance:** Running a company entails adopting most of the best practices in your chosen industry. What this means is that you should play by the rules, since each industry has its unique set of regulatory requirements. These are applied in company leadership, shareholder rights, executive salary package, and director nomination. To avoid being punished by governmental agencies that watch over businesses' activities, you should never try tax avoidance or corruption, and you should operate transparent internal control. Carry out your business' audit periodically as necessary and map out simple and definite ways to fight cybersecurity and other external threats to your business's survival.

11.2 Entrepreneurs Aren't Machines

Entrepreneurs aren't machines. You can read that five times until it really sinks into your subconscious mind. It is inspiring to become an entrepreneur, but it is stress-inducing to run your business in a dangerous way where you pay little or no attention to self-care.

Hustling and bustling (or grinding), as they call it in entrepreneur circles, is fine as long as you constantly remind yourself that your health comes first before every other thing. Health is wealth; if you are too sick or indisposed to manage a business, it will fail. That should be seen as double losses and entrepreneurs should avoid that at all costs.

When you set aside time to look after yourself and your health, you will be physically and mentally strong to manage all your tedious day-to-day business activities. More so, you will enjoy absolute clarity, concentration, and experience increased creativity, productivity, and less stress.

Do the following and you will be physically and mentally fit to handle all aspects of your entrepreneurship with ease:

- **Sleep well:** It is estimated that an adult requires an average of 6-8 hours to totally rejuvenate their bodies. Good sleep helps streamline the metabolic activities in the human body. Imagine how powerful and refreshed we feel after waking up from a good sleep! Unfortunately, some entrepreneurs don't respect their own bodies; they work all round the clock. Such people are only putting themselves through avoidable burnout. In the end, they will lose on both fronts by losing their businesses as well as their health!

- **Eat well:** Good food and balanced diets will supply your body with the much-needed nutrients so that you can remain healthy all time to handle the routine affairs of your business.

- **Keep a good cycle of friends and relations:** It is strongly advisable that you keep the company of people that are able to uplift or motivate you in various ways. In addition to your family and friends, entrepreneurs are known for hobnobbing with other business owners. There are a lot of things to gain from networking with other entrepreneurs; you can learn new approaches to running your business and have the opportunity to meet mentors who have done exactly what you are trying to do.

- **Focus on personal development:** As your business grows, you will need to regularly update your skill sets so that you will be able to manage new challenges. Every entrepreneur should learn a little more about these three main skills required for managing a company:

    1. **Accounting and/or financial skills:** No one expects you to know everything about accounting, but at least you are required to know your numbers. This indicates that you must have a fundamental knowledge of how much you are spending and how much money your business is making.

    2. **Communication and interpersonal skills:** Running a business involves effective and objective communication. You should be able to know how to rally people, most especially, your employees around your projects. More so, you should facilitate interpersonal communication among the people working in your company.

    3. **Project management skills:** You need to constantly update your knowledge about project management so that you can equip yourself with the latest approaches for executing projects in your business.

- **Build your spirituality or religious belief:** Everything a human being does revolves around their spiritual belief. If you are the type who believes every achievement you have received in your business is divinely ordained, it pays to regularly build and maintain your spiritual belief in order to remain perfectly aligned or attuned to your overall being.

11.3 Ethics, Standards, and Regulations (Obey all the Laws of the Land)

As an entrepreneur, you are not running your company in a vacuum. There are laws, ethics, standards, and regulations put in place by governmental agencies in the jurisdictions where your businesses are located to guide you and other business owners.

It is your sole responsibility as a business owner to obey all the laws of the land for your own good. These laws may vary from one location to another. No one expects you to study law before you could know which laws are applicable to your business operations. You can learn from those who are operating in the same industry as you. Even local business bureaus or agencies can guide you in identifying which standards, regulations, and laws your business needs to pay attention to. If you can afford it, having a few hours' consultation with an attorney can save you a lifetime of embarrassment and regret if law enforcement agents show up in your company to discover that you have been flouting all the necessary laws.

Here are some of the laws that may or may not be applicable to your business/industry:

- **Intellectual property laws:** Laws about patents and trademarks

- **Business tax laws:** The laws guiding all the requirements about income tax, employment tax, and excise tax.

- **Employment laws:** These include the Fair Labor Standards Act (FLS, Equal opportunity laws, Workers' compensation, Family and Medical Leave Act, Occupational Safety and Health Act, Americans with Disabilities Act, and Equal Pay Act.

- **Health-care laws**

- **Advertising laws**

- **Privacy laws**

- **Finance laws**

11.4 Business Bootstrapping

As an entrepreneur, you wear many hats. If your business is self-funded and new, you may act as the accountant, attorney, bookkeeper, human resource person, and marketer because you may not have the funds to hire people. Yet, as part of running a business, all these functions have to be covered. So, how is it possible to bootstrap owning a business while keeping your sanity? Read on.

The first rule of thumb is to operate the business with the minimum amount of expenses. When first starting out, working in a space that does not require rent is the way to go. You may also use equipment that is donated or sold at a discount to not burn a hole in your pockets. Learning basic accounting and making an excel spreadsheet to track the money coming into the business and going out of the business is a great way to monitor and manage finances without the services of an accountant or bookkeeper. Researching the laws and regulations for operating your business, and staying in compliance allows for covering the legal aspects of running the business without an attorney.

Marketing a business can be a huge expense, but as someone bootstrapping the business, you look for ways to spread the work inexpensively. Using social media to post announcements about the product or service and the delightful stories of happy clients or customers saves on the expense of marketing or hiring a marketer. There might even be a way to partner for cross-promotion of your product and service. Find a business owner that has a business similar to yours and make an agreement to promote their product or service and they promote your products or services in return. For example, one of the business owners has a resume-writing service and the other business owner has an interview prep service. Each of them wants more clients so they agree to include the website of the other business owner in their blogs.

Bootstrapping a business takes sacrifice, research, and determination to succeed. They are the core of operating a start-up. Sacrificing the money in your savings to self-fund the start-up is a short-term pain for a long time gain. As someone bootstrapping a business, you need to be your own accountant and attorney until you have the cash flow to hire them. So, until you can hire them, you need to take the time to know how to record the finances and balance the books. You will also need to take the time to learn what legal regulations you need to be in compliance with as you start and grow your business. In addition to learning the financial and legal aspects of owning a business, while bootstrapping, being creative with marketing is a must. Finding creative methods of marketing such as free social media marketing, cross-promotions, and customer referral programs saves a great deal of money and time. When starting a new venture such as owning a business, the more people on your side and supporting you the better!

Quiz

1. **What does ESG stand for?**

   a. Economic, social, and government

   b. Environmental, social, and governance

   c. Educational, social, and governance

2. **This is NOT one of the reasons a company needs to embrace the concept of corporate sustainability.**

   a. To utilize renewable or recyclable raw materials

   b. To protect the environment

   c. To fight its competitors

3. **The environmental aspect of corporate sustainability requires that a business_____**

   a. should not protect the environment

   b. should not use renewable sources of energy

   c. should reduce pollution

4. **Entrepreneurs are machines; they should overwork themselves.**

   a. True

   b. False

   c. I don't know

5. **For personal development, an entrepreneur needs to**_____

   a. believe that he/she knows everything about how to run a company

   b. upgrade his/her skills by learning from others (mentors)

   c. forget about improving his/her communication skill

6. **When you pray and express your faith in a higher, divine power, you are** _____

   a. Developing your management skill

   b. Building up your faith/belief

   c. Learning some financial skills

7. **Which of these skills isn't necessary for an entrepreneur?**

   a. Accounting/financial skill

   b. Interpersonal communication skill

   c. Dancing skill

8. **What is the responsibility of a business owner as far as the social aspect of corporate sustainability is concerned?**

   a. Having good company leadership

   b. Reducing pollution

   c. Having good and fair labor relations

9. **A sensible entrepreneur doesn't need one of these social groups.**

   a. Mentors

   b. Supporting business associates

   c. Binge-drinking and hard-partying friends

10. **All of these are the benefits an entrepreneur can enjoy from regular self-care except_____**

    a. great mental health

    b. physical fitness

    c. poor level of creativity

Answers	1 – b	2 – c	3 – c	4 – b	5 – b
	6 – b	7 – c	8 – c	9 – c	10 – c

Chapter Summary

◆ Both an entrepreneur and his/her business can drop dead or collapse if he/she fails to take good care of himself/herself

◆ Entrepreneurs are not machines; this means that they should consider doing some self-care procedures that may include eating good food, sleeping well, connecting with the right people, and engaging in personal development.

◆ To run a company that has ample chance of surviving, an entrepreneur needs to strictly improve on these three factors enabling corporate sustainability: Environmental, social, and governance factors.

◆ There are laws, ethics, standards, and regulations that entrepreneurs need to strictly abide by in whatever jurisdiction they are running their businesses.

References

- Boss Project (2017, March 16). The importance of self-care as an entrepreneur. Available at: www.bossproject.com

- Galante, M. (2021, November 15). Crucial business laws for entrepreneurs. Available at: www.squareup.com

- One Trust (2021, June 18). The ultimate guide to ESG management and factors. Available at: www.onetrust.com

- Tarver, E. (2022, August 18). 5 skills every entrepreneur should have. Available at: www.investopedia.com

Chapter **12**

Exit Strategy

It is a fact that not all entrepreneurs have the desire to run their businesses forever. Due to certain circumstances beyond their control, entrepreneurs may decide to exit their own companies/businesses for good. For example, when an entrepreneur becomes too old or incapacitated to run the day-to-day operations of his/her business, the most sensible action is to exit it. Or if the co-founders are a married couple and are going through a feisty divorce, one of them (or both of them) may choose to exit the business. Nowadays, we have people who are called "serial entrepreneurs". This category of entrepreneurs would start a new business, grow it for some years, and then sell (exit) the business and make some profits from the sale.

Intrinsically, there are seven common exit strategies for entrepreneurs, and they are all discussed in this chapter

Key learning objectives should include the reader's understanding of the following

- Passing the business to a successor

- Ownership transfer through management or employee buyout

- Selling the business to a third party

- Mergers and Acquisitions (M&As)

- Initial Public Offering (IPO)

- Liquidation and close

- Filing for bankruptcy

12.1 Passing the Business to a Successor

For most owners of small-and-medium-sized businesses, the best route for exiting their companies is to pass the management and, sometimes, the ownership of those businesses to their children, reliable relations, or to someone they trust to successfully manage the business' affairs.

Before handing over the management of the company to their family members, most entrepreneurs would have requested that their family members join the company as employees and systematically learn about how the company is operated.

As simple as this process appears, it may be a little complicated if there have already been some grievous misunderstandings among the family members inheriting the company. There may be disagreements on who should become the CEO of the company and what percentage of ownership each family member can lay claim to. This is why it is advisable that the parent (entrepreneur) transferring the ownership to his/her offspring should stipulate in a legally binding document(s) who owns what and what position each of them should occupy in the company.

More so, transferring a property (like a company) has some tax issues. In the US, an entrepreneur can transfer his/her company to his/her children either in the form of a gift/present or an estate. It could be transferred as a gift when the entrepreneur is still alive, and such an entrepreneur would only be taxed based on the difference in the fair market value (FMV) of the company. On the other hand, if the entrepreneur has passed away, the company would be transferred to his/her children as an estate, and the new owners of the estate will be required to pay taxes on the estate.

The concept of FMV entails that if a company is worth $50 million, but the owner decided to hand it over to his/her family members for free ($0) or a little amount of money, say $5 million, the entrepreneur (owner of the business) will be asked by Internal Revenue Service (IRS) to pay tax on the difference between $50 million and $5 million, which is $45 million.

When passing a company's ownership to family members, it is mandatory to inform the IRS about this change of ownership, stipulating who will be henceforth responsible for paying taxes on the company's business activities.

This approach is also applicable to passing a company's ownership to a charity. Now, the law passed in 2018 makes it possible for charitable organizations to hold 100% of a company's equity or ownership. Since charities are not taxed, it is the responsibility of the entrepreneur giving the business to pay the applicable taxes. So, if you are giving your company to a charity as a gift in the US, you will not be required to pay capital gains tax. However, if you are selling the company to a charity above the company's cost or worth, even though it is less than fair market value, you will surely be asked by the IRS to pay capital gains tax.

12.2 Ownership Transfer Through Management or Employee Buyout

It is possible for an entrepreneur to transfer the absolute ownership (100% ownership) to its employees or existing management of the company after they have agreed, in principle, to outright purchase the company. Some founders of small- and medium-sized companies adopt this approach to hand over the reign of their businesses to trusted managers and employees who they might have worked with for several years.

When this happens, the tax responsibilities of the company shift to the new owners. The seller of the business may only be expected to pay a one-time capital gains tax.

12.3 Selling the Business to a Third Party

This is a straightforward approach for entrepreneurs to exit their businesses. In this scenario, they are not relinquishing the ownership of their employees, family members, investors, or existing managers in the company. They are outright selling the business to a third party, which could be a competitor or another entrepreneur.

One of the merits of adopting this method is that it summarily eliminates the issue of conflict of interests. There could be a serious instance of conflict of interest if you are selling your company to your employees, current investors, or family members. More so, you may be persuaded to sell the business for less than it is worth in the market.

At the same time, you could rest assured that in case the business fails in the near future, it won't, in any way, affect your relationship with the buyer/new owner. Imagine selling your business to your brother, son, or friend and it eventually collapses; the fallout from such a deal/transaction could destroy the erstwhile robust relationship you've ever had with the new owner who happened to be your brother or so.

As soon as the sale of the business is finalized, all tax responsibilities attached to the business are passed onto the new owner's shoulders.

12.4 Mergers and Acquisitions (M&As)

This is the process whereby two or more companies agree, in principle, to combine their resources in order to create a larger corporate entity. There are some advantages for undertaking mergers and acquisitions, such as having the opportunity to command a huge percentage of the market, achieving increasing profitability, and diversity into different industries or making different products without the hassles of setting up new, expensive manufacturing plants.

For example, the $65 billion American Online and Time Warner deal in 2001 didn't succeed. Similarly, in 2012, Google partnered with Motorola in a deal estimated at $12.5 billion, but each company later went their separate ways when the partnership didn't materialize.

As an entrepreneur, due to the low success rate of M&As, it may be advisable that you choose another more successful route to exit your business. This doesn't mean that some M&As don't succeed. However, make sure you have all the facts and data before opting for an M&A exit strategy.

12.5 Initial Public Offering (IPO)

An entrepreneur may take his/her business public through Initial Public Offering (IPO). The public will be allowed to own chunks of the business by purchasing the company's stocks/shares.

It is important to know that an IPO can be mostly conducted for medium-sized and large companies that have been in operation for some years. It may take a business anywhere between 8 and 10 years from founding before it can be ready for an IPO.

Nowadays, the fastest way to IPO a company is through SPAC, which is an acronym for Special Purpose Acquisition Company. A company can be founded today and merged with another company that is already publicly traded. So, the new company automatically becomes a subsidiary of the existing parent company, and can easily raise money through the parent company by issuing shares that shareholders can publicly buy or trade.

In the course of time, an entrepreneur can exit his/her publicly traded company by selling all his/her shares in the company.

Since the process of doing an IPO involves a series of complex documentation, an entrepreneur may require the service of an investment banker and accountants to help them draw up and execute a realistic IPO plan.

12.6 Liquidation and Closure

When a business is underperforming and is mostly in debt, the business owner can liquidate all its holdings and shut it down permanently.

Sometimes due to a rapid change in an industry and apparent loss of market/customers, a company may find it very difficult to remain in business. In that circumstance, the owner may decide to close it.

When liquidating your business in the US, pay attention to the following important information. According to IRS, these are the required steps an entrepreneur is expected to take while closing his/her business:

- **File a final return and related forms:** You are required to file your company's final return and fill in all the necessary information required in related forms. You may also need to complete additional documentation depending on each state's requirements.

- **Take good care of your employees:** You are expected to timely pay all their salaries and accruing benefits before closing your business. This includes making sure that their retirement savings/contributions are being paid for.

- **Pay your taxes:** If you owe the IRS any taxes and other state's taxes, it is advisable that you should endeavor to pay all of them before liquidating your company. If you don't have enough money to settle all those taxes at once, you could make an arrangement with the IRS and other related tax agencies.

- **Report your contract workers:** IRS requires that business owners report all payments made to their contract workers before shutting down their business operations.

- **Cancel your EIN and close your IRS Business Account:** You'll be asked to cancel your EIN and discontinue your IRS Business Account.

- **Keep your business records in a safe place:** For future reference, it is advisable that you keep all your business records in a safe place. You may need to consult them sometime in the future.

12.7 File for bankruptcy

When faced with insurmountable financial woes, an entrepreneur can elect to file for either Chapter 7 or Chapter 11 bankruptcy.

The main difference between the two approaches is that Chapter 7 will liquidate the company's assets if it cannot pay its debts. On the other hand, Chapter 11 bankruptcy allows the business to continue to be in operation, but under a reorganization plan.

For Chapter 11 bankruptcy, a court-appointed receiver manager or organization or committee will oversee the affairs of the bankrupted company to prevent its assets from being sold off, leaving investors and shareholders in the lurch.

NOTE:

Whichever approach you are adopting to exit your company, pay attention to both the federal and state laws, because these laws are different from state to state.

Quiz

1. **Which of these exit strategies is not generally applicable to a small business?**

   a. Initial Public Offering (IPO)

   b. Succession

   c. Outright sale to a third party

2. **One of these issues could derail an exit by succession.**

   a. If the company has no products to sell

   b. If the company has many customers

   c. If the family members in the succession process have previous misunderstandings

3. **What does SPAC stand for?**

   a. Special Purpose Acquisition Company

   b. Special People Association Center

   c. Special Paper Account Code

4. **What is the idea behind SPAC?**

   a. A new company can raise funds from the public as a subsidiary of its parent company

   b. To deceive shareholders

   c. To avoid paying IRS taxes

5. **Which of these agencies is responsible for collecting federal taxes in the US?**

   a. Federal Reserve

   b. Bank of America

   c. Internal Revenue Service (IRS)

6. **If an entrepreneur is still alive while passing his company to his children for no charge, this is referred to as...**

   a. gifting

   b. charitable contribution

   c. estate transfer

7. **Which of these professionals would be required when preparing an exit via IPO?**

   a. A warehouse manager

   b. An investment banker

   c. A security personnel

8. **What happens when an entrepreneur is selling his/her company to a charity?**

   a. The entrepreneur must pay a capital gains tax when he/she sells at the company at a higher price

   b. The entrepreneur doesn't need to pay any taxes

   c. The entrepreneur cannot sell his/her business to a charity

9. **According to the law passed in 2018, a charity can now hold how much percentage equity in a business?**

   a. Only 20%

   b. Only 5%

   c. 100%

10. **Chapter 7 bankruptcy entails that a company absolutely.... when it can no longer service its debts.**

    a. liquidate its assets

    b. reorganize its assets

    c. do nothing about its condition

Answers	1 – a	2 – c	3 – a	4 – a	5 – c
	6 – a	7 – b	8 – a	9 – c	10 – a

Chapter Summary

◆ There are seven possible ways an entrepreneur can exit his/her business: By succession, ownership transfer to employees/managers, Initial Public Offering (IPO), liquidating/closing the business, merger & acquisition, selling the business to a third party, or filing for bankruptcy.

◆ An entrepreneur can elect to pass the company to his/her children as a "gift" while he/she is still alive; otherwise when he/she passes away, the company can be inherited by his/her children in the form of an "estate".

◆ Whichever approach an entrepreneur takes to exit his/her business, it is important that he/she should consider all the necessary documentation and taxes involved in the chosen process.

◆ It is important to check the different tax requirements from state to state; sometimes, some states in the US have their own specific tax requirements that must be complied to while exiting a company.

◆ Entrepreneurs need some help from investment bankers and/or accountants when doing an IPO or merger or acquisition.

References

- Wood, M. (2020, November 19). 8 business exit strategies for you to consider. Fundera. Retrieved from www.fundera.

- OrgMapper (2023). Why do mergers and acquisitions fail: The 12 most common reasons. Retrieved from www.orgmapper.com

- Segal, T. (2022, May 24). Corporate bankruptcy: An overview. Investopedia. Retrieved from www.investopedia.com